THE AMAZING BOOK OF ORIGAMI

A STEP-BY-STEP ILLUSTRATED GUIDE TO MAKING MODELS BY USING THE CREATIVE ART OF PAPER FOLDING

JON TREMAINE

TIGER BOOKS INTERNATIONAL
LONDON

Credits

Photography
Neil Sutherland

Editor
Philip de Ste. Croix

Designer
Stonecastle Graphics Ltd.

Production
Ruth Arthur
Sally Connolly
Neil Randles
Karen Staff
Jonathan Tickner

Director of production
Gerald Hughes

Typesetting
Stonecastle Graphics Ltd.

Colour reproduction
HBM Print PTE Ltd,
Singapore

Printed and bound in Italy by
Poligrafici Calderara, S.p.a.
Bologna

CLB 3546
This edition published 1994 by
Tiger Books International PLC,
London
© 1994 CLB Publishing,
Godalming, Surrey
ISBN 1-85501-542-0

THE AUTHOR

Jon Tremaine was originally introduced to origami in the 1950s by the legendary Robert Harbin, long recognized as the "father of British origami". Jon was one of the founder members of the British Origami Society and is a regular contributor to the Society's magazine. He lectures and demonstrates origami to local organizations and at conventions throughout the United Kingdom. A professional magician for more than 30 years, Jon is also the author of the titles on magic and card tricks in this series. He is a member of London's Inner Magic Circle, and has been honoured by them with a Gold Star, the highest award that a magician can receive. He is the author of a set of four books about performing magic specifically for children – the series is entitled "Let's Make Magic". He is married and lives in Cuckfield, Sussex.

INTRODUCTION

Paper is one of the first things we are given to play with as children. Often nothing fascinates us more than a clean, blank sheet of paper. We seem compelled to do something with it. Artists want to draw and paint on it, writers want to cover it with words, magicians want to do tricks with it, and origami devotees want to fold it into three-dimensional shapes. All four groups want to create something out of nothing. I am a magician, writer, artist and origamaniac! All four! That is why I love paper so much. This book will teach you how to fold beautiful paper models – the fascinating, almost magical art of Origami.

The first recorded folded paper models were made in China. When you realize that the Chinese invented paper in the first place, this is not really surprising. The Japanese invented the art in the 8th century and it has held an important place in both religious and secular life in that country ever since.

My mother taught me my first origami fold – a Paper Dart. You will find it recreated for you later in this book. Most people learn a fold or two from their parents. All the models in this book (with a few indicated exceptions) are folds that have been handed down from generation to generation through the ages, traditional folds whose origins are shrouded in the mists of time. I have been collecting them for over thirty years and it is a delight for me to record some of them in this book.

When I was eighteen years old I became a member of the Magic Circle and I met a wonderful magician – the late Robert Harbin. He pioneered the resurgence of origami in the western world, and gave me my first origami lesson. He taught me to fold the marvellous Flapping Bird that you will find later in this book. It is a traditional Japanese design and one of the most perfect ever devised. Once you have successfully folded a Flapping Bird you will be hooked on origami for life. Robert was a master of origami and created many new models which he generously shared with fellow folders through his many published books and television shows. During our many meetings Robert went to great pains to explain to me the importance of studying folding techniques and classical folds. He taught me that only through a thorough knowledge of these principles can you ever hope to create new models.

Origami has come a long way since those days in the early 1960s. The British Origami Society was formed in 1967 and is widely respected by origami enthusiasts the world over. If, after reading this book, you become hooked on origami and want to progress further, contact the B. O. S. or one of the other origami societies whose addresses you will find below.

A universal sign language has been developed that will enable you to pick up an origami book written in a language that you do not understand and yet still manage to fold the models that it describes, simply by following the internationally recognized symbols. I introduce you to these symbols on pages 12 and 13 of this book. You will soon get the hang of it as I guide you through the simple rules.

You may be tempted to open the book somewhere in the middle and start with one of the models that you find there. *Avoid the temptation* because I have graded the models so that you learn new folding skills as you go. So take it step by step, because the models increase in their degree of difficulty as you progress through the book.

Do not panic if a fold foxes you to begin with. Look ahead to the *next* illustration in order to examine the position that you are trying to achieve. Examine it carefully and then try again. Soon you will be producing marvellous models. This book will introduce you to a wonderful hobby. Young or old, it will give you endless hours of therapeutic entertainment. I hope you come to enjoy it as much as I do.

ORIGAMI SOCIETIES

Australia
Australian Origami Society
2/5 Broome Street
Highgate
Perth 6000

Japan
Nippon Origami Association
1-0960 Domir Gobancho
12 Gobancho, Chiyodaku
Tokyo 102
Japan

Great Britain
British Origami Society
11 Yarningale Road
Kings Heath
Birmingham
B14 6LT

U.S.A.
The Friends of The Origami
Center of America
15 West 77th Street
New York, NY 10024-5192
U.S.A.

PAPER

Almost any paper will do. Japanese origami paper is best, but wrapping paper, paper bags, envelopes with interesting linings, computer paper are all fine – really any paper will do as long as it is not too thick, takes a crease well, and does not easily split when you fold or refold it. Many types of Japanese origami paper are produced. The most common is generally coloured on one side and is either white or an entirely different colour on the other. Traditionally patterned and textured papers are also great fun to experiment with.

If you do not live and shop in a major town, you will find Japanese origami paper quite hard to find. You will need to look in a good quality arts and crafts or specialist paper craft shop. There are a few Japanese craft shops dotted about the U.K. They should hold a useful stock as well as a selection of books. If you experience problems locating origami, paper write to Janet Wilson of Paper Magic, 34 Purfield Drive, Wargrave, Berks, RG10 8AR, or write to one of the national origami societies listed on the previous page. They will be able to supply your needs by post and will send you a product and price list plus a few samples.

Origami paper can work out quite expensive. For that reason I practise my folds on lesser quality paper and, when I feel that I have mastered the fold, I will select a better quality sheet of paper of a type that I feel will best reflect the character of the model. Most stationery shops sell jotter blocks of 1,000 sheets of either white or coloured paper sized 10cm x 10cm. I find these very useful for practice work.

Try to be neat with your folds. Make your creases firm and your points accurate. The more care you take, the better will be your end result. Origami follows geometrical lines and is very precise. The purist origami exponents frown on the use of scissors. They say that your end result should be achieved by folding, and folding alone. I tend to agree with them in general terms. However, I see nothing wrong with the inclusion of a cut if the result that you are seeking cannot be achieved in any other way. For example, the ears and buck teeth on my "Floppy Ears Rabbit" could not have been so impressively produced without a cut. I have to admit that I approach my origami in the same way that I approach my magic. I like to use the simplest method to achieve my goal, and I am not interested in unnecessary technicalities. Thus my work is easier to teach. Thankfully the wonderful Japanese folders Isao Honda and Kunihiko Kasahara seem to agree with me and are not averse to including a cut or two in their work.

MAKING A SQUARE FROM AN OBLONG

If you are asked to start with a square piece of paper it is very important that you check that it *is* absolutely square. You will soon find yourself in trouble if it is not!

(**1**) Fold the diagonal so that the top edge aligns with the left hand side of the paper.

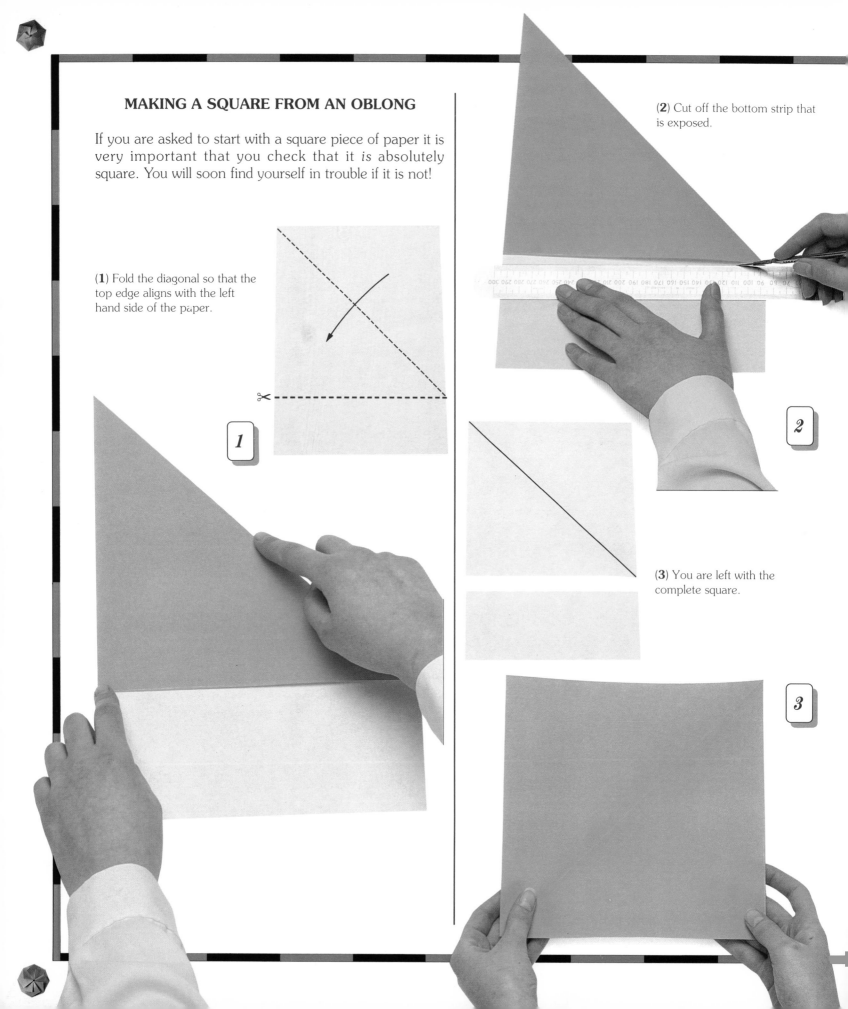

(**2**) Cut off the bottom strip that is exposed.

(**3**) You are left with the complete square.

MAKING AN EQUILATERAL TRIANGLE

All three sides of an equilateral triangle are the same length. This is how you produce one. Start with an oblong piece of paper. Fold it in half horizontally and then open it out again.

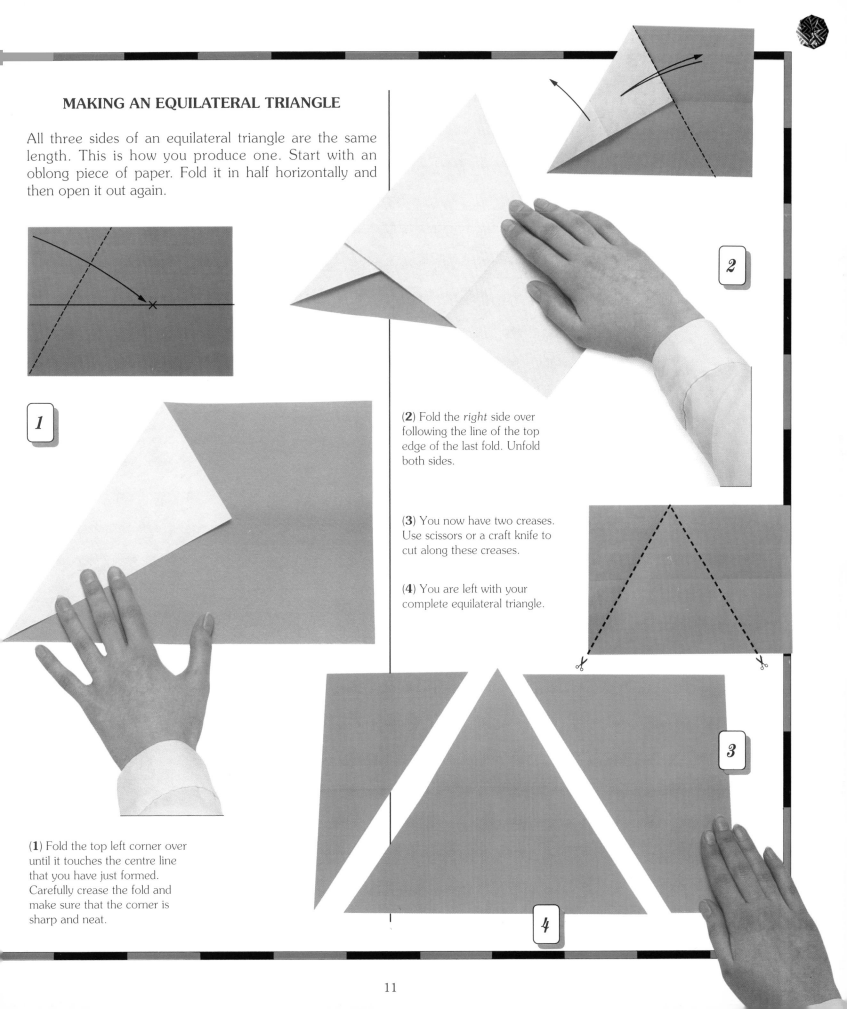

(**2**) Fold the *right* side over following the line of the top *edge* of the last fold. Unfold both sides.

(**3**) You now have two creases. Use scissors or a craft knife to cut along these creases.

(**4**) You are left with your complete equilateral triangle.

(**1**) Fold the top left corner over until it touches the centre line that you have just formed. Carefully crease the fold and make sure that the corner is sharp and neat.

11

THE FOLDING SYMBOLS

In the 1960s a Japanese genius named Akira Yoshizawa devised a system of symbols that he used to describe the method of folding the hundreds of new models that he was creating. This system has now been universally adopted. It is very easy to learn and quite logical.

(**1**) **Valley fold.** When opened it looks like a valley.

(**2**) **Mountain fold.** The opposite to a valley fold.

(**3**) **Cut along here.** A scissors symbol with a bold dash line.

(**4**) **Existing crease.** A thin unbroken line.

(**5**) **Previous position or X-Ray view.** A faint dotted line.

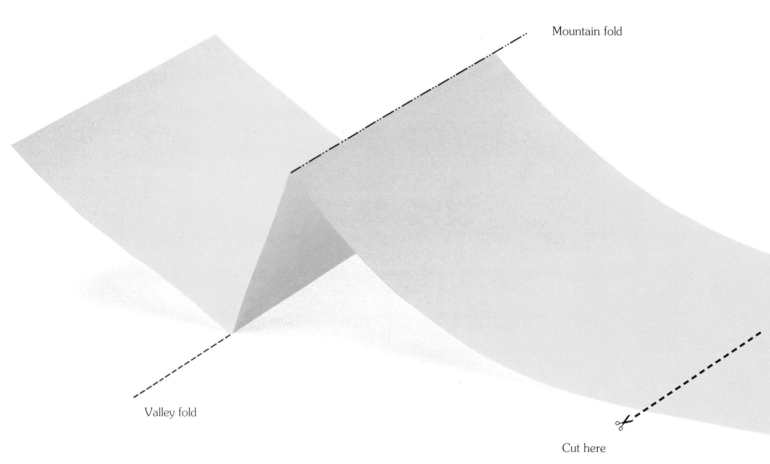

Mountain fold

Valley fold

Cut here

(6) Hold here. The circle marks the spot where you should hold the model.

(7) Watch this spot. The **X** helps you to keep track of a particular corner when you look at the *next* illustration. Letters of the alphabet are used when more than one spot has to be kept track of.

(8) Fold in front. Usually a valley fold.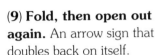

(9) Fold, then open out again. An arrow sign that doubles back on itself.

(10) Fold behind. A white-headed half-arrow.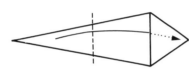

(11) Tuck in. Often used for locking a model.

(12) Open out. Open up previously folded parts as directed.

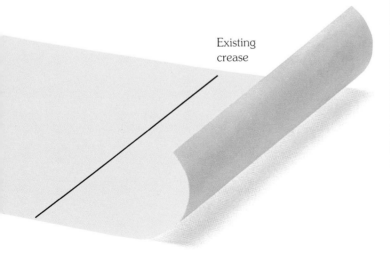

Existing crease

(13) Apply force. Press or push in the required direction.

(14) Fold over and over. Like a flattened roll.

(15) Turn model over. Either from top to bottom or side to side, as directed by the arrow.

(16) Rotate. The arrow shows you how far and in what direction you should turn the model.

(17) Enlarged view. A larger view is often needed to illustrate minute details of a fold.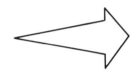

(18) Accordion pleat. A row of alternating valley and mountain folds.

(19) Inflate. Some models have to be blown up. This "puff" arrow shows you where to blow.

(20) Distances are equal. Used for clarity when an uneven number of similar folds are used.

(21) Repeat same fold. A similar fold has often to be repeated with similar flaps or corners. The number of cross bars on the body of the arrow tells you how many repeat folds to do.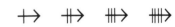

(22) Bring together. Two parts must be pulled or joined or sometimes glued together.

FOLDING TECHNIQUES

There are a few basic folding techniques that you should learn. They are all very easy. Grab an odd piece of paper and practise the following:

INSIDE REVERSE FOLD

(**1**) Valley fold the paper in half. Hold where shown with your right finger and thumb and push upwards at the "push" symbol with your left thumb.

(**2**) The left half of the paper is turned in on itself and reversed.

(**3**) The creases are sharpened and the inside reverse fold is complete.

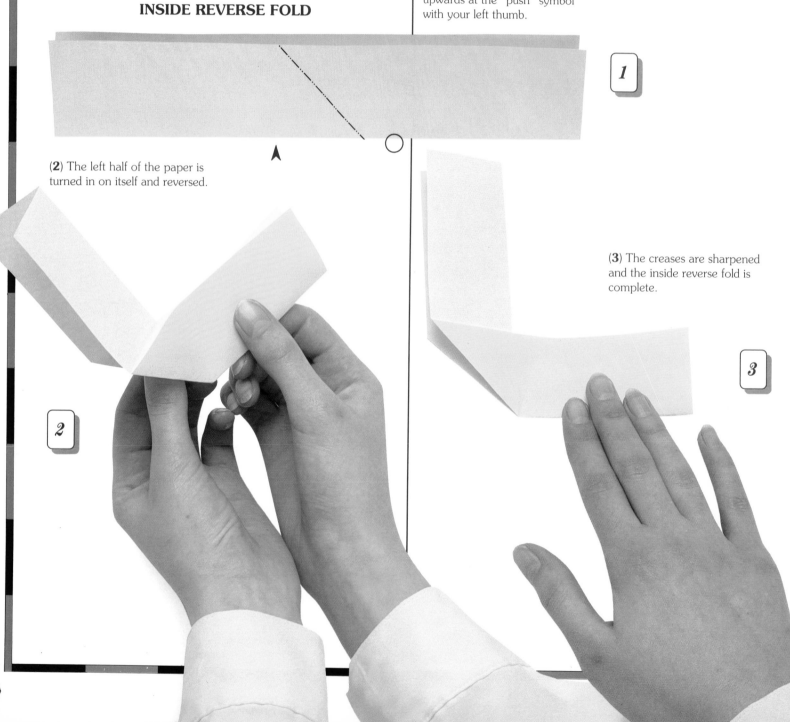

OUTSIDE REVERSE FOLD

(**1**) Valley fold the paper in half.

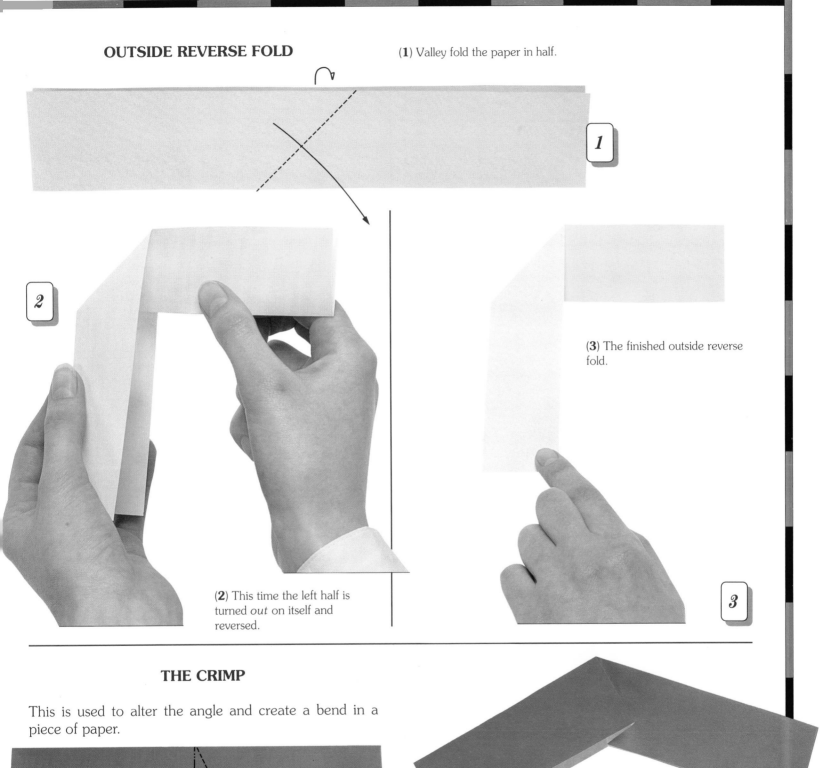

1

2

(**2**) This time the left half is turned *out* on itself and reversed.

(**3**) The finished outside reverse fold.

3

THE CRIMP

This is used to alter the angle and create a bend in a piece of paper.

(**1**) Make the mountain and valley folds illustrated.

1

2

(**2**) Push across and flatten the paper into the new position. This is called a crimp.

RABBIT'S EAR

This is a very commonly used fold.

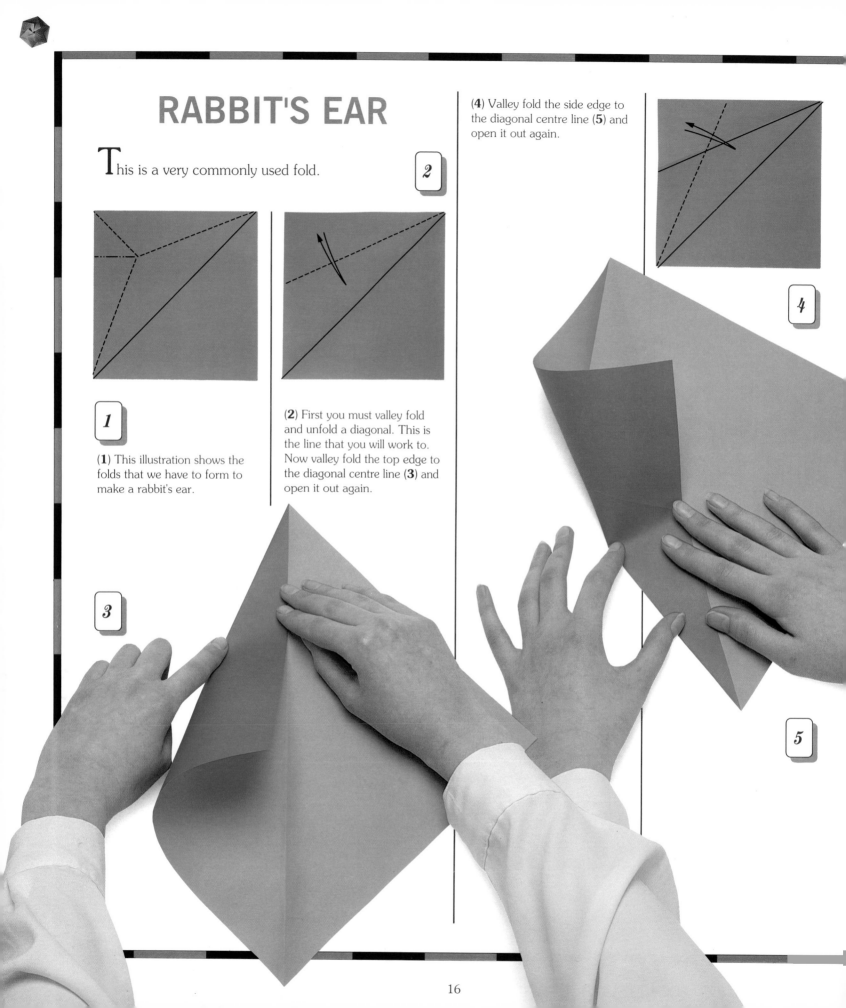

(4) Valley fold the side edge to the diagonal centre line (**5**) and open it out again.

(1) This illustration shows the folds that we have to form to make a rabbit's ear.

(2) First you must valley fold and unfold a diagonal. This is the line that you will work to. Now valley fold the top edge to the diagonal centre line (**3**) and open it out again.

16

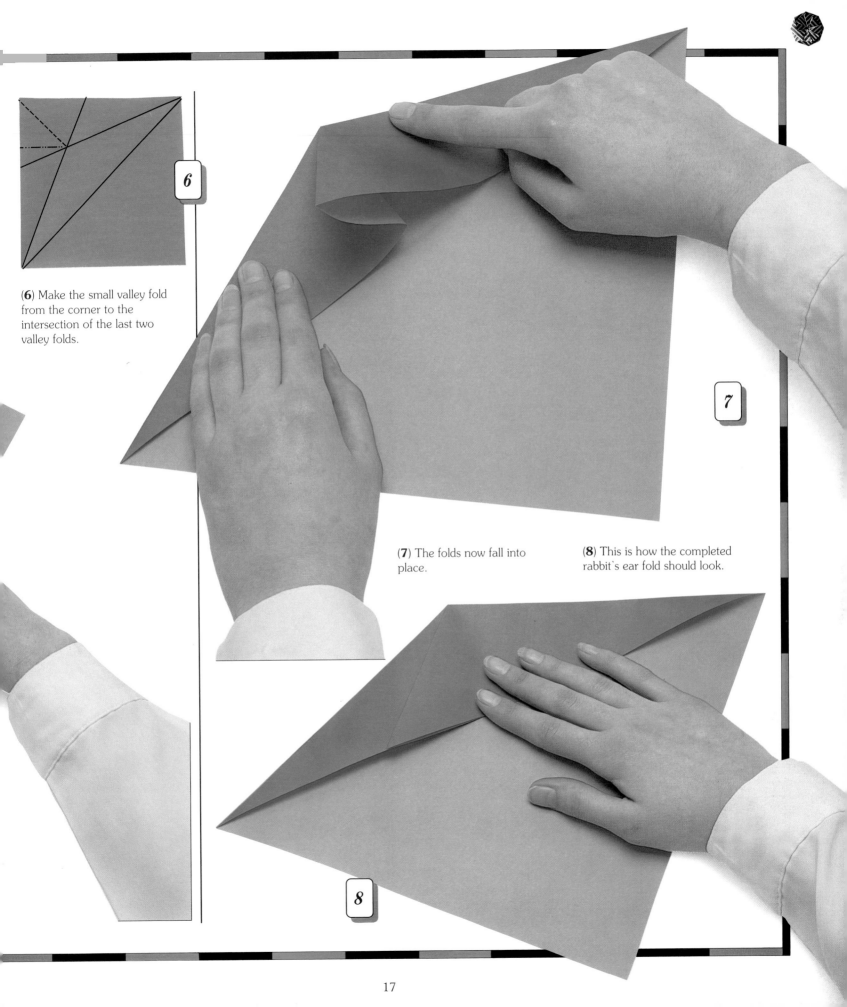

(**6**) Make the small valley fold from the corner to the intersection of the last two valley folds.

(**7**) The folds now fall into place.

(**8**) This is how the completed rabbit's ear fold should look.

THE BASES

There are a handful of bases – basic folds – from which the majority of the models in this book are formed. I propose to describe them all in this section so that you can refer back to them as required. This saves me having to repeat myself over and over again and gives us more space in the book for the models. The bases are all easy to learn and you will soon find that you are able to fold them *without* having to refer back to these pages. All the bases start with a square piece of paper.

THE PRELIMINARY FOLD

The bird and frog bases that follow both start off with the preliminary fold.

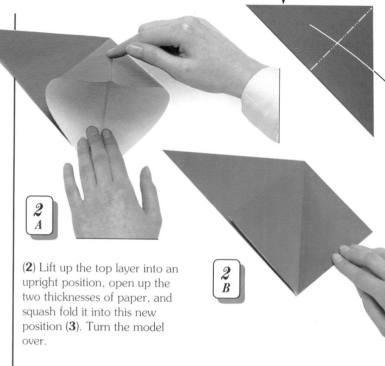

(**2**) Lift up the top layer into an upright position, open up the two thicknesses of paper, and squash fold it into this new position (**3**). Turn the model over.

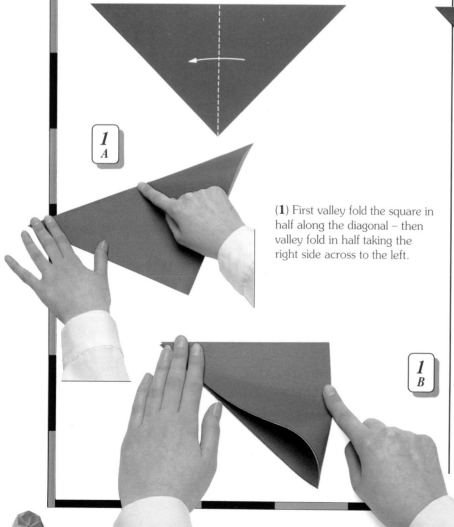

(**1**) First valley fold the square in half along the diagonal – then valley fold in half taking the right side across to the left.

(**4**) Repeat the squash fold on this side.

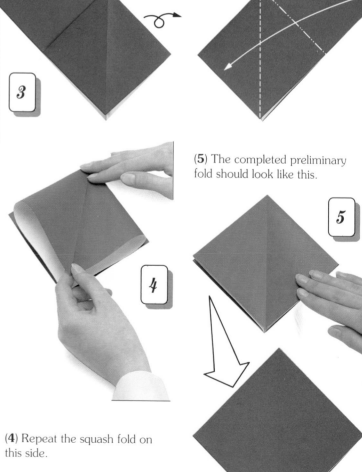

(**5**) The completed preliminary fold should look like this.

THE BIRD BASE

Start with the preliminary fold.

(**1**) Lift up the first thickness of the fold and take it upwards and forwards. Watch where point "X" ends up. At the same time push in the sides as indicated.

1 A

1 B

(**2**) Press the folds carefully and try to make nice crisp points. Now repeat with the flap at the back.

2

(**3**) Valley fold the upper flaps downwards, front and back.

3

(**4**) The completed bird base looks like this.

4

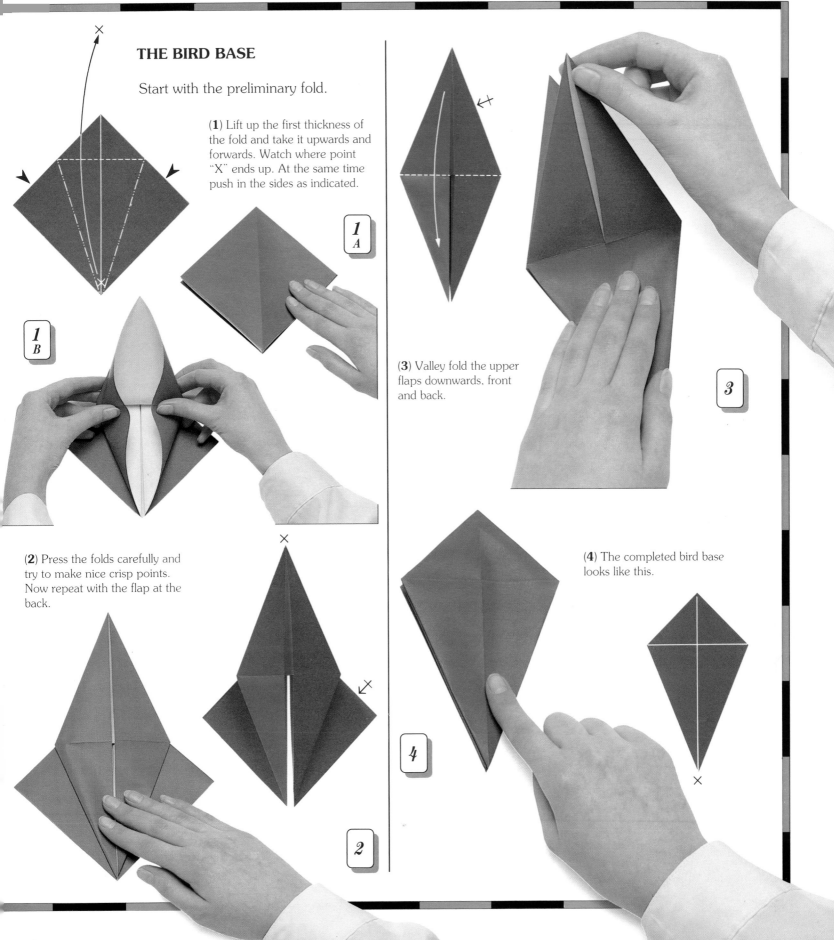

THE FROG BASE

Start with the preliminary fold.

(**1**) Raise the top right hand flap into an upright position and press where shown.

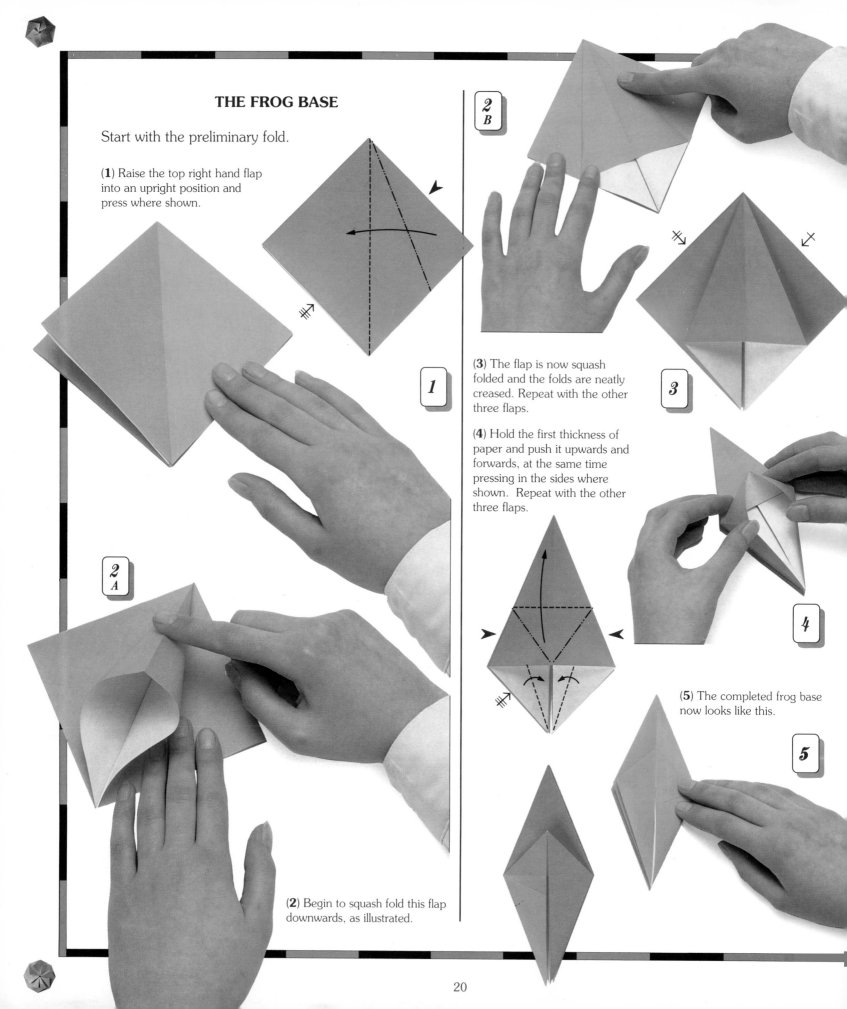

(**2**) Begin to squash fold this flap downwards, as illustrated.

(**3**) The flap is now squash folded and the folds are neatly creased. Repeat with the other three flaps.

(**4**) Hold the first thickness of paper and push it upwards and forwards, at the same time pressing in the sides where shown. Repeat with the other three flaps.

(**5**) The completed frog base now looks like this.

THE DIAMOND BASE

First fold a diagonal across the square of paper which you will work to.

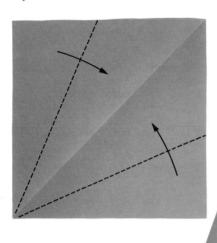

(**2**) Valley fold both the right and top edges of this kite shape, again to the centre diagonal.

(**1**) Valley fold both the left and bottom edges to the centre diagonal crease.

(**3**) By doing this, you have completed the diamond base.

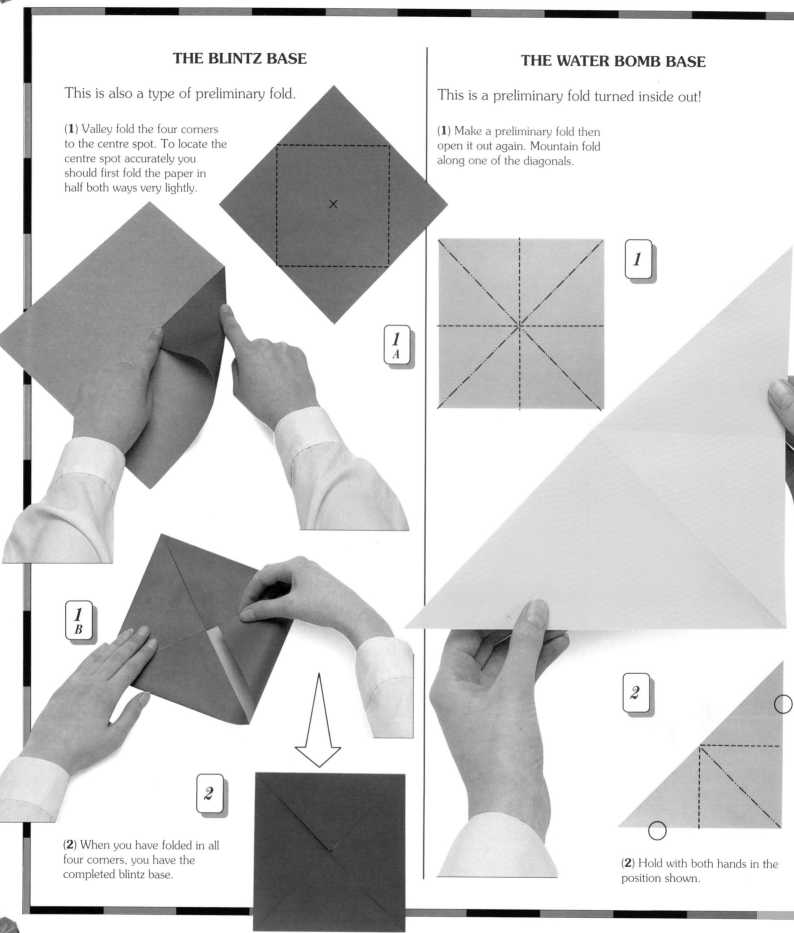

THE BLINTZ BASE

This is also a type of preliminary fold.

(**1**) Valley fold the four corners to the centre spot. To locate the centre spot accurately you should first fold the paper in half both ways very lightly.

1 A

1 B

2

(**2**) When you have folded in all four corners, you have the completed blintz base.

THE WATER BOMB BASE

This is a preliminary fold turned inside out!

(**1**) Make a preliminary fold then open it out again. Mountain fold along one of the diagonals.

1

2

(**2**) Hold with both hands in the position shown.

THE FISH BASE

Start with the diamond base.

(1) Lift out the two hidden corners and push them forward.

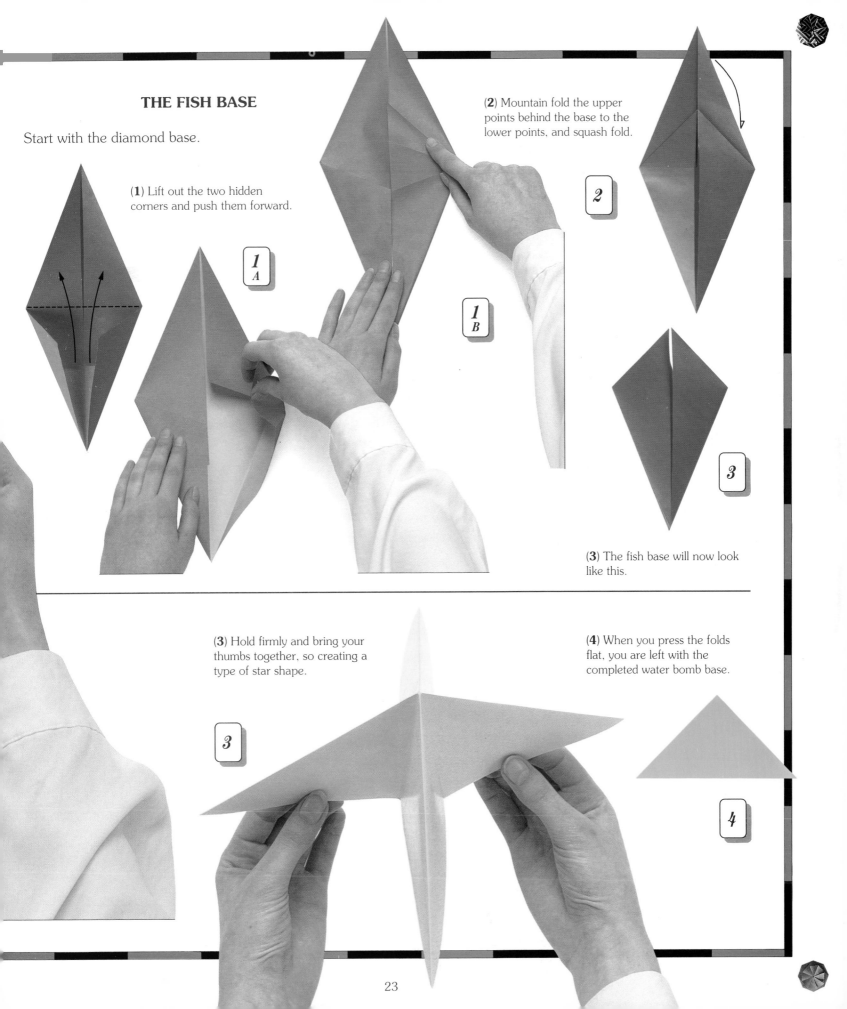

(2) Mountain fold the upper points behind the base to the lower points, and squash fold.

(3) The fish base will now look like this.

(3) Hold firmly and bring your thumbs together, so creating a type of star shape.

(4) When you press the folds flat, you are left with the completed water bomb base.

COMMON FOLDS

THE SQUASH FOLD

You will have already done a couple of these, but I include it here for clarity and completeness. Start with a water bomb base.

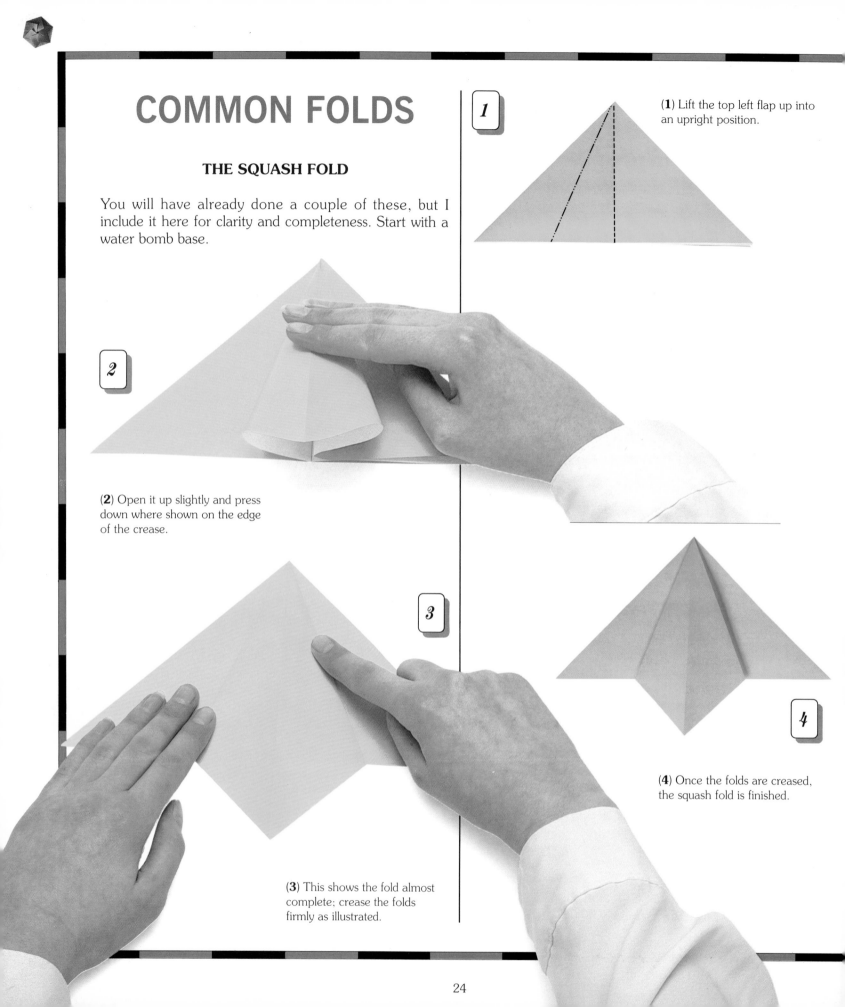

1

(**1**) Lift the top left flap up into an upright position.

2

(**2**) Open it up slightly and press down where shown on the edge of the crease.

3

4

(**4**) Once the folds are creased, the squash fold is finished.

(**3**) This shows the fold almost complete; crease the folds firmly as illustrated.

THE PETAL FOLD "A"

For this fold you should carry on from the squash-folded water bomb base that you have just practised.

(1) Lift up the bottom corner and push it upwards and away from you. Press in the sides where shown. Watch corner "X".

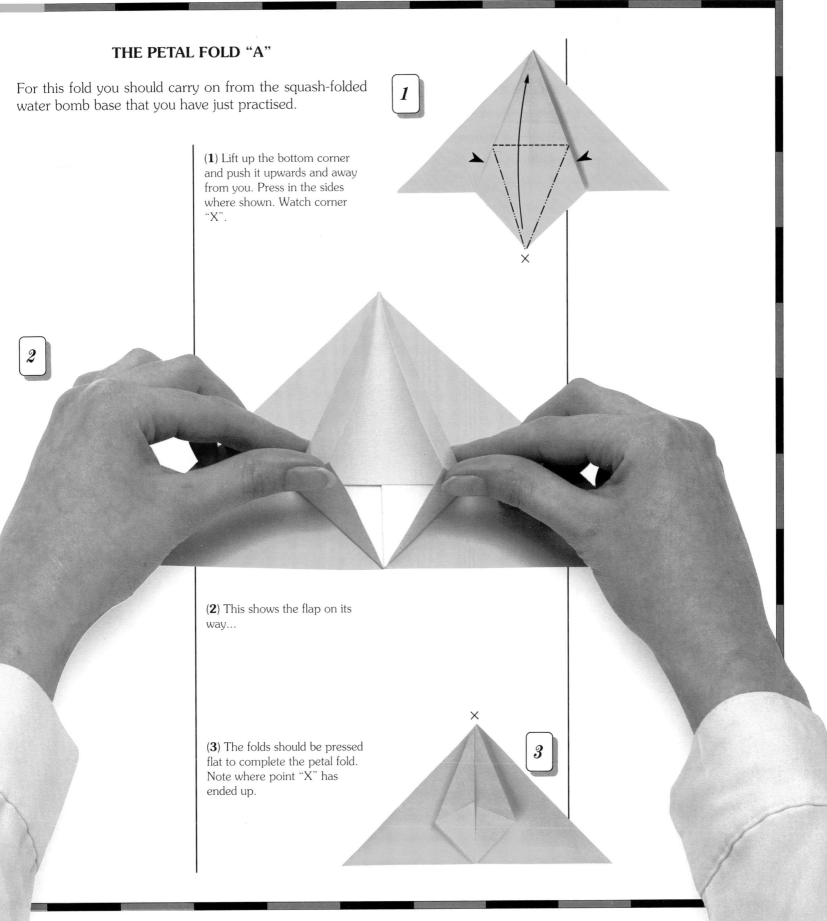

(2) This shows the flap on its way...

(3) The folds should be pressed flat to complete the petal fold. Note where point "X" has ended up.

THE PETAL FOLD "B"

This is similar to the above petal fold. For the purposes of this example, we are working with the frog base.

(**1**) Lift the top flap and push it upwards and forwards, pressing in the sides as you do this. Watch point "X".

1

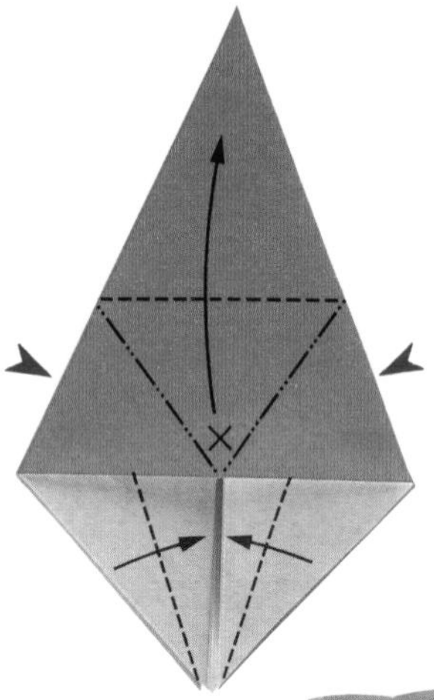

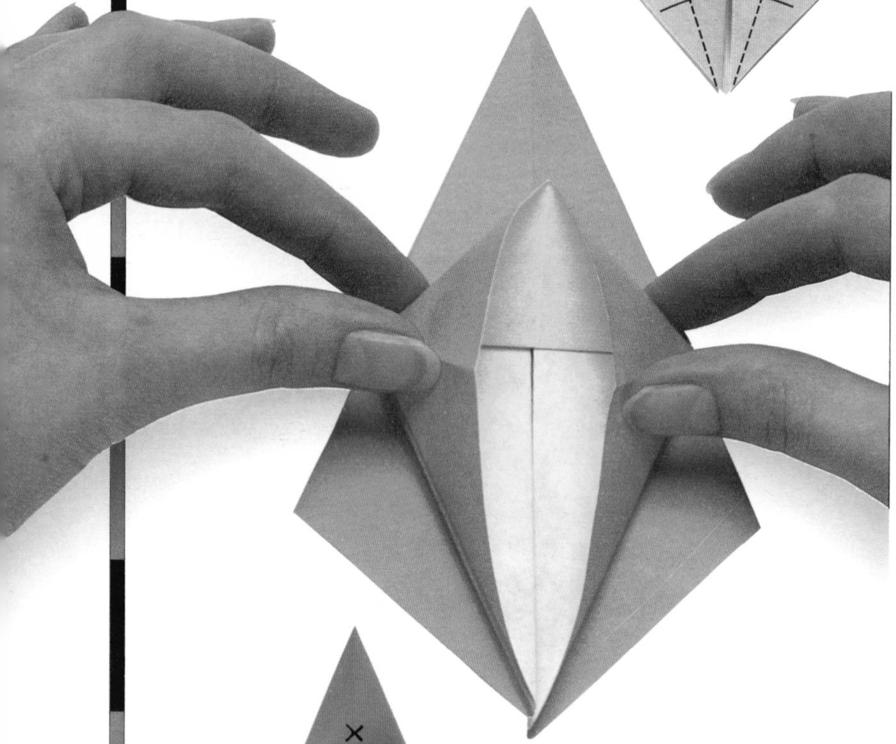

2

(**2**) The completed petal fold looks like this.

THE BOOK FOLD

(**1**) Valley fold the paper in half across the vertical axis. That is all there is to it!

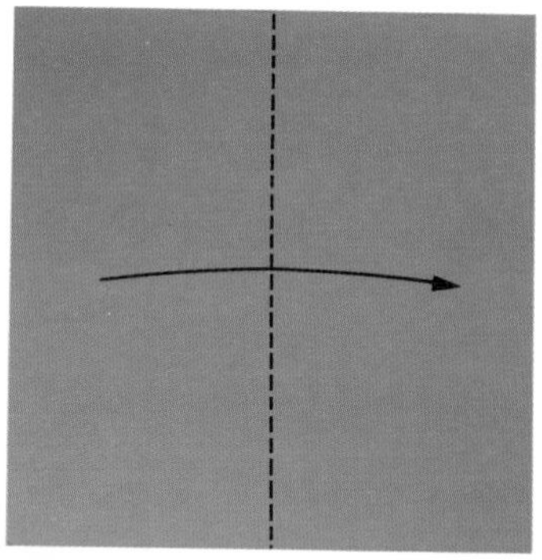

1

SINKING

This is a bit more difficult but do not panic! Start with the preliminary fold.

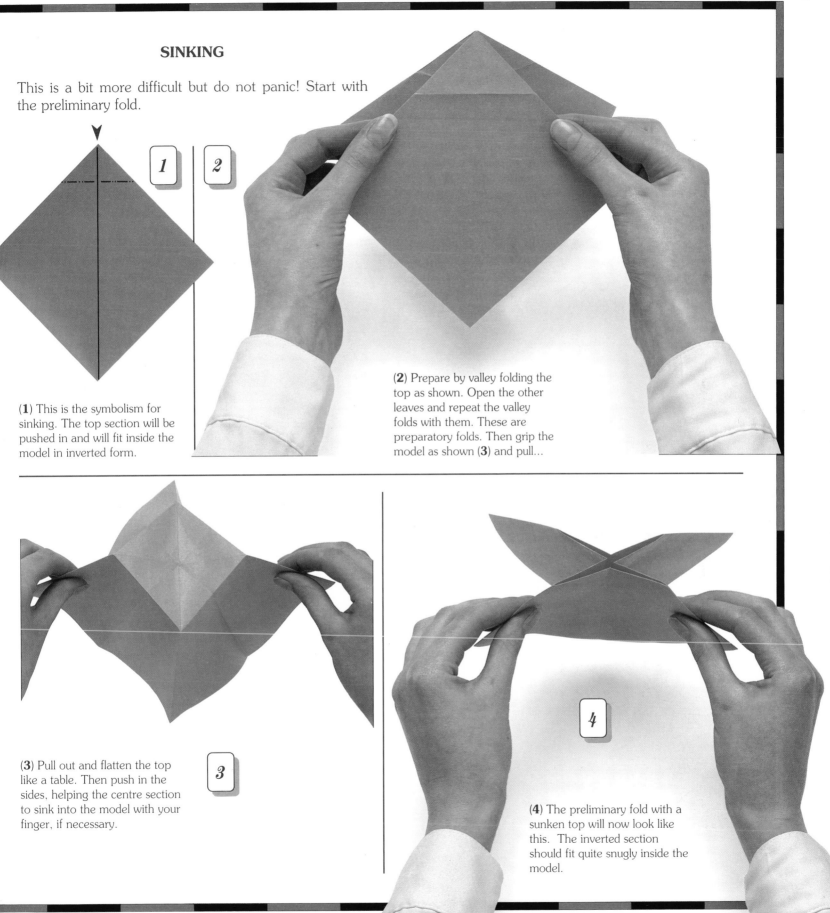

1

2

(**1**) This is the symbolism for sinking. The top section will be pushed in and will fit inside the model in inverted form.

(**2**) Prepare by valley folding the top as shown. Open the other leaves and repeat the valley folds with them. These are preparatory folds. Then grip the model as shown (**3**) and pull...

(**3**) Pull out and flatten the top like a table. Then push in the sides, helping the centre section to sink into the model with your finger, if necessary.

3

4

(**4**) The preliminary fold with a sunken top will now look like this. The inverted section should fit quite snugly inside the model.

PAPERWORK

THE PAPER DART

This is probably everyone's introduction to origami. Can you ever forget the thrill of launching your first paper dart in the classroom, and the horror you felt as it headed for the teacher! My mother taught me this version – the first origami model I actually made. Use a square of paper. Lay it coloured side down.

(**1**) Valley fold the paper in half along its vertical axis and open it up again.

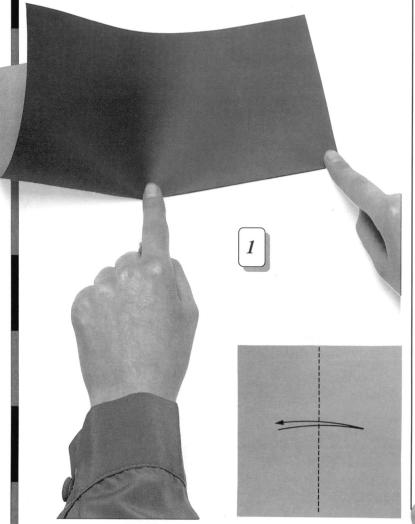

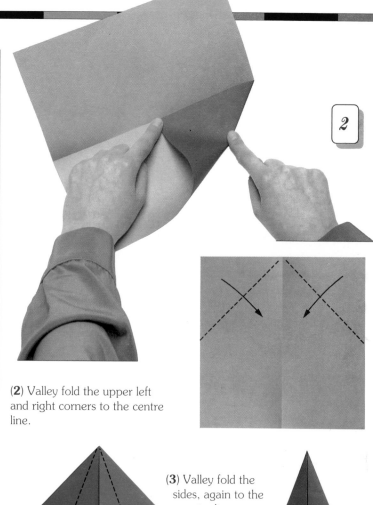

(**2**) Valley fold the upper left and right corners to the centre line.

(**3**) Valley fold the sides, again to the centre line.

(**4**) Turn the model over.

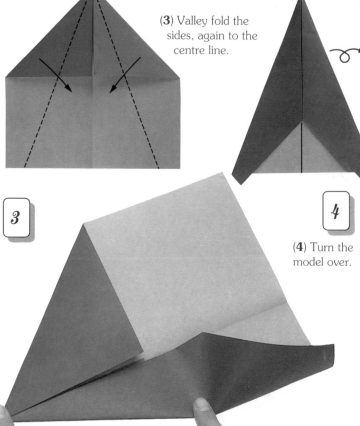

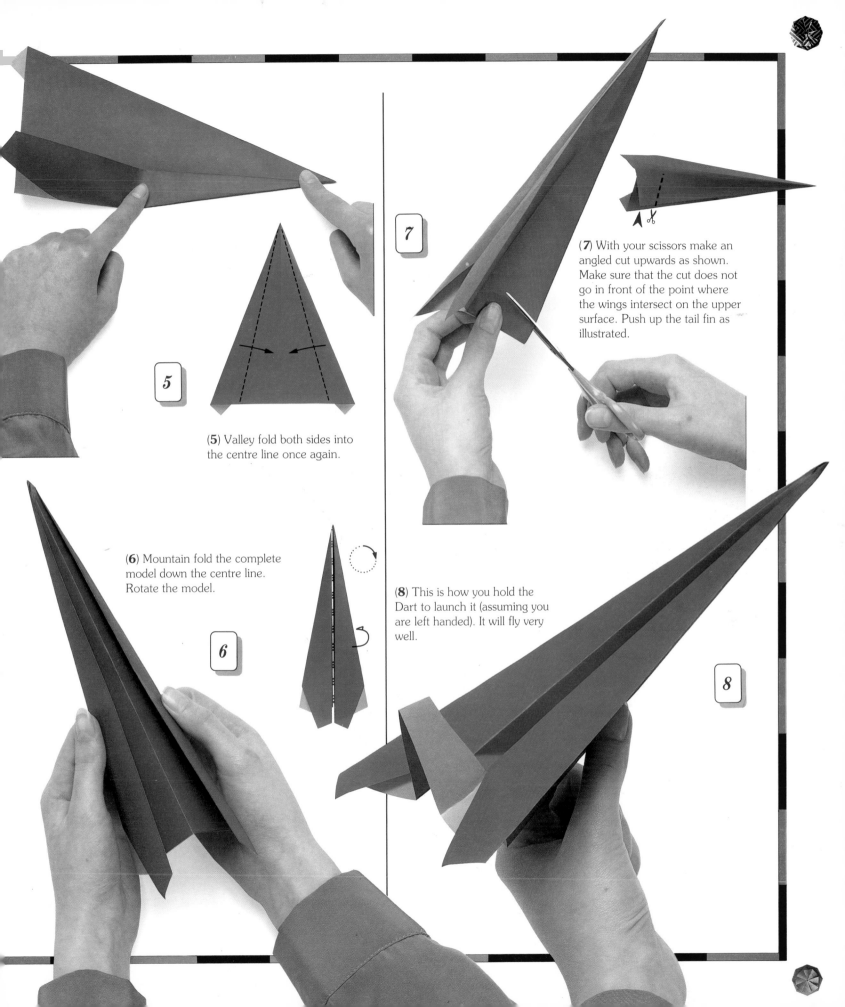

(5) Valley fold both sides into the centre line once again.

(6) Mountain fold the complete model down the centre line. Rotate the model.

(7) With your scissors make an angled cut upwards as shown. Make sure that the cut does not go in front of the point where the wings intersect on the upper surface. Push up the tail fin as illustrated.

(8) This is how you hold the Dart to launch it (assuming you are left handed). It will fly very well.

THE MULTIFORM

Robert Harbin called this next series of traditional folds the Multiform. One surprise follows another and different figures keep appearing. I will start you off with the Salt Cellar. Use a square of paper – coloured side down.

(**1**) Pre-crease the paper with vertical, horizontal and diagonal valley folds. Now fold in the four corners to meet at the centre point.

(**2**) You have made a blintz base. Turn the model over.

(**3**) Valley fold the four corners in to the centre point.

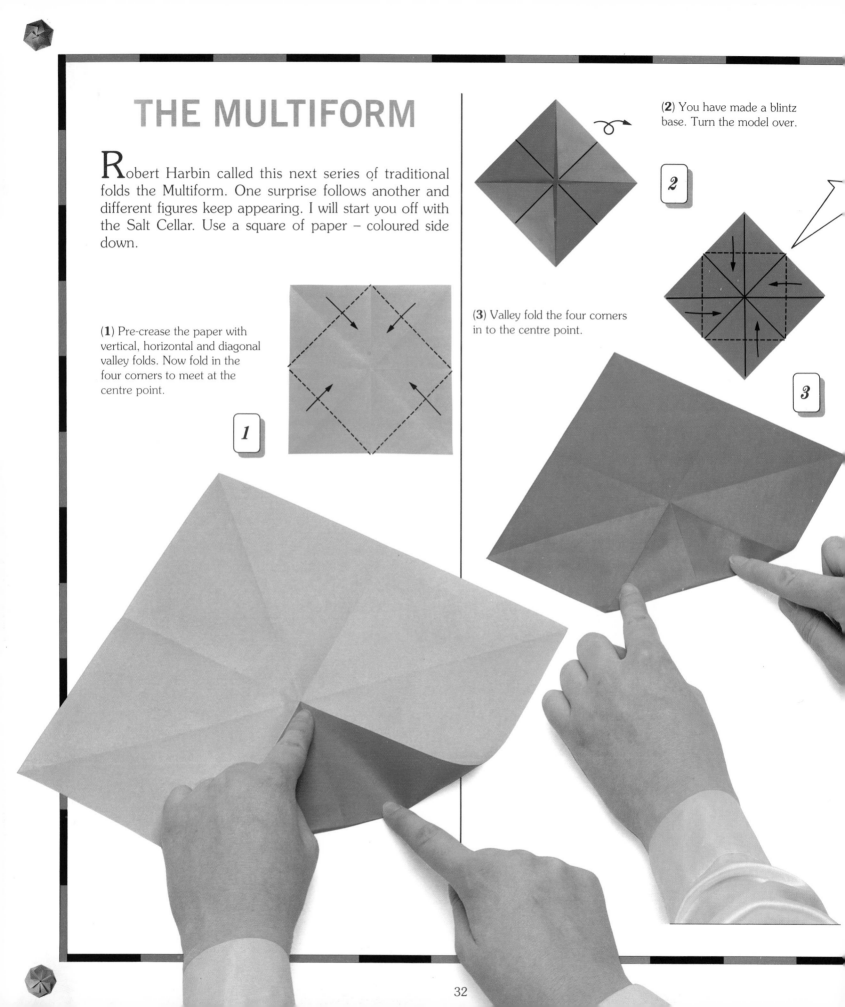

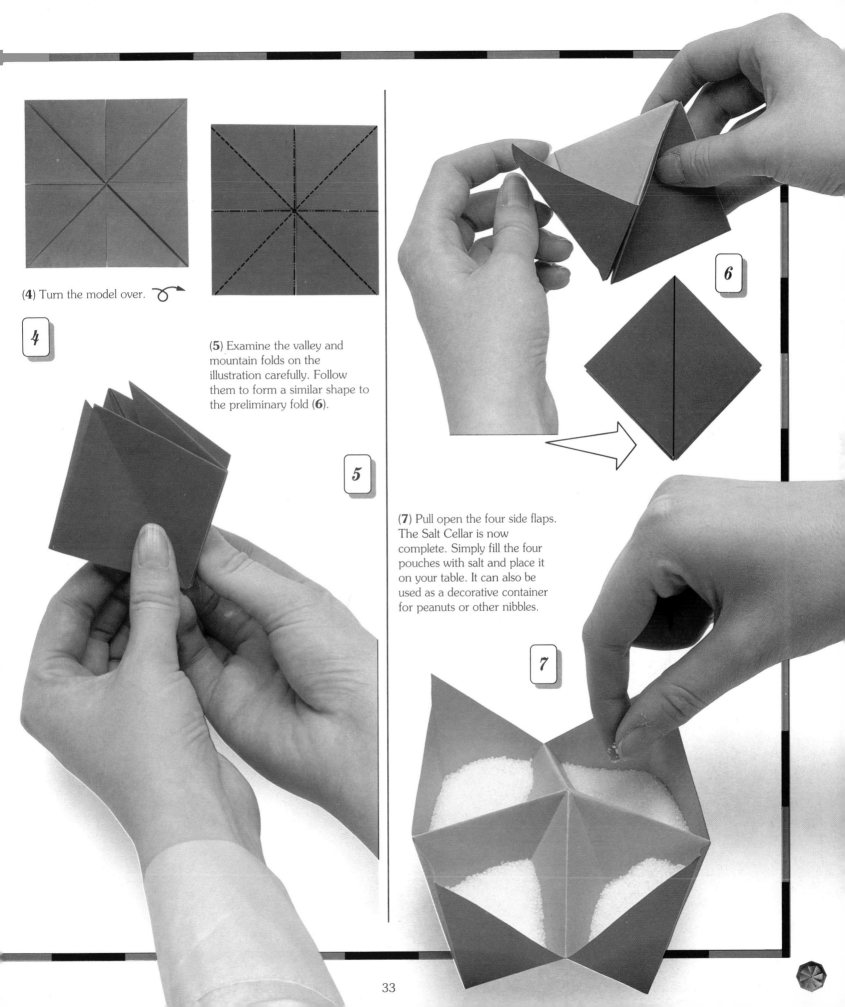

(**4**) Turn the model over.

4

(**5**) Examine the valley and mountain folds on the illustration carefully. Follow them to form a similar shape to the preliminary fold (**6**).

5

6

(**7**) Pull open the four side flaps. The Salt Cellar is now complete. Simply fill the four pouches with salt and place it on your table. It can also be used as a decorative container for peanuts or other nibbles.

7

THE CATAMARAN

Originally a Tamil word for a float made of logs roped together, the catamaran – or twin-hulled yacht – is now a common sight in marinas around the world. This is a traditional Japanese version. Start with position (**5**) of the Salt Cellar.

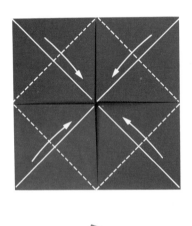

(**1**) Valley fold the four points to the centre.

1

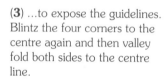

(**3**) ...to expose the guidelines. Blintz the four corners to the centre again and then valley fold both sides to the centre line.

3

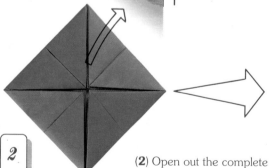

2

(**2**) Open out the complete model...

(**4**) Mountain fold the model in half across its horizontal axis.

4

(**6**) Pull out a corner and draw it across, to make a pointed bow shape.

6

(**5**) Valley fold the lower flaps upwards, front and back.

5

(**7**) Fix in this new position by pressing in the creases. Repeat with the other three points, and you have made the Catamaran.

7

THE WINDMILL

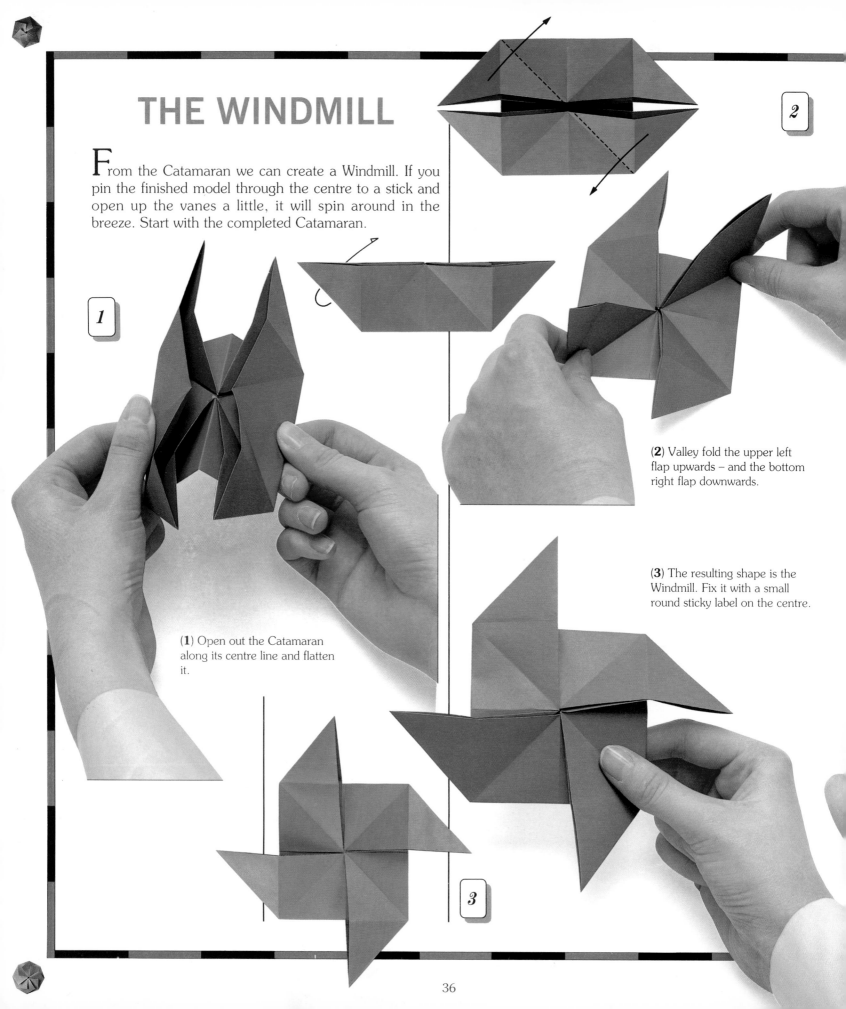

From the Catamaran we can create a Windmill. If you pin the finished model through the centre to a stick and open up the vanes a little, it will spin around in the breeze. Start with the completed Catamaran.

2

1

(**2**) Valley fold the upper left flap upwards – and the bottom right flap downwards.

(**3**) The resulting shape is the Windmill. Fix it with a small round sticky label on the centre.

(**1**) Open out the Catamaran along its centre line and flatten it.

3

THE SEAT OR VASE

From the Windmill we progress to making a Seat or (depending on how you look at it) a Vase. This very stylized model is a typical Japanese design. Start with the completed Windmill.

(**2**) Valley fold across the diagonal. Rotate the model through 90°.

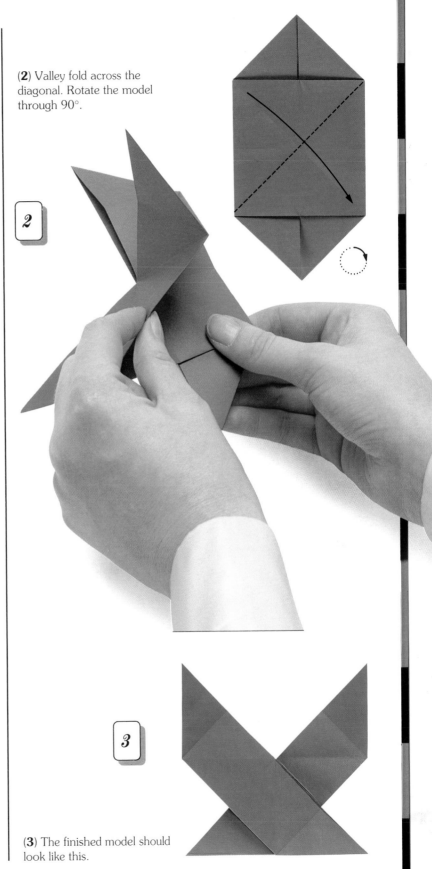

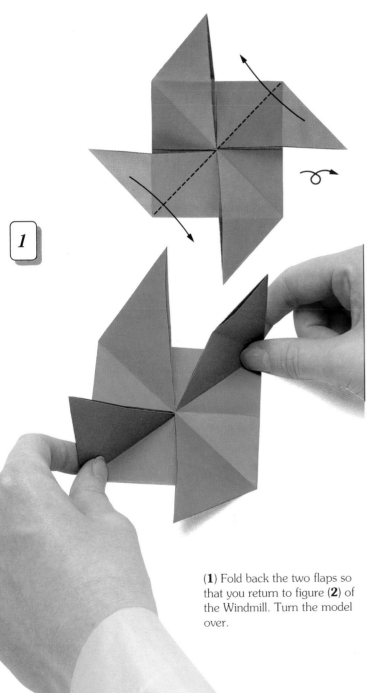

(**1**) Fold back the two flaps so that you return to figure (**2**) of the Windmill. Turn the model over.

(**3**) The finished model should look like this.

THE BOAT WITH SAIL

With just a little twist your Seat can become a Boat. If you make this from waterproof paper it should float – ideal for bathtime! Start with the finished Seat.

(**1**) Valley fold the right hand leg across to the left. Rotate the model through 90°.

1 A

1 B

2

(**2**) Lo and behold, the Boat with Sail!

THE PAJARITA

We can use our Boat to set sail for Spain to discover their best-known fold, the Pajarita. This is Spanish for "Little Bird". It is also a general word used by the Spanish to describe origami. Most Spanish children are conversant with this fold. In some countries this fold is known as the Hobby Horse.

(**1**) Start with the Boat with Sail. Outside reverse fold the right half downwards.

(**2**) Rotate the model through 180°

(**3**) The Pajarita is revealed. By bending open the front legs slightly, your bird will sit up for you.

THE CONTAINER

For our final variation on the Multiform design, let's go back a bit – to the Catamaran. From this we can create a very stylish Container, which you can use to hand round sweets, peanuts, etc, or in which you can keep small objects, like pins or paperclips. Start with the finished Catamaran.

1

(**1**) The Catamaran is our starting point for this model.

(**2**) Reach inside the back wall of the Catamaran, which is of double thickness. You will find a point. Gently pull this outwards and upwards.

2

3

(**3**) This is how the model should look. Now pull out the equivalent flap on the other side...

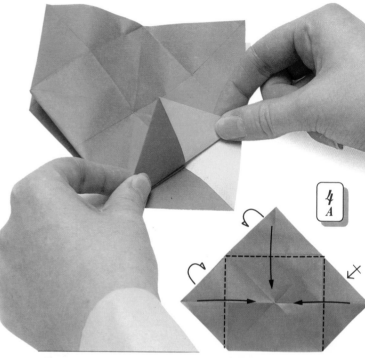

4 A

4 B

(**4**) Valley fold the top and two sides to the centre. Repeat behind.

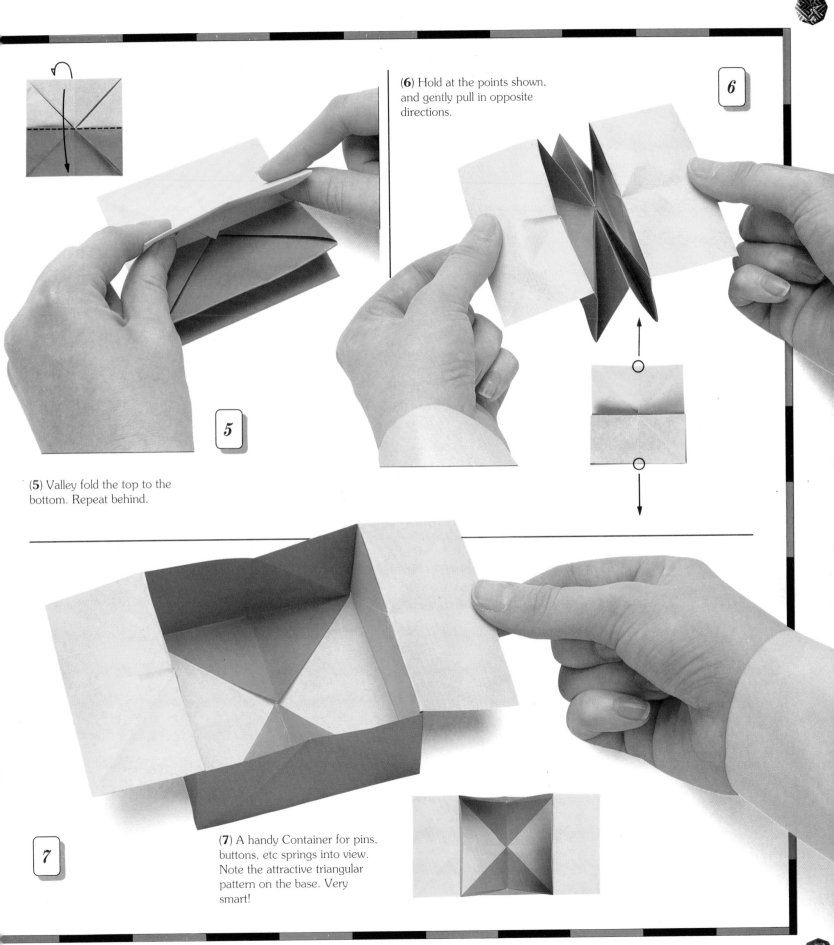

(**6**) Hold at the points shown, and gently pull in opposite directions.

6

5

(**5**) Valley fold the top to the bottom. Repeat behind.

7

(**7**) A handy Container for pins, buttons, etc springs into view. Note the attractive triangular pattern on the base. Very smart!

YAKKO-SAN

In Japan there is a traditional clown known as Yakko-San. This cute little character has long been a favourite with paper folders. This fold has been passed down through the generations since the 13th century. Yakko-San has got a very large head and wears a kimono. Looking up his sleeves a child will be delighted to find Yakko-San's pointed hands. You will soon discover that he is a blood relative of all our previous models. Use a square of paper.

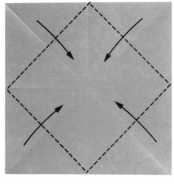

(**1**) Prefold the vertical, horizontal and diagonal crosses. Valley fold in the four corners to the centre point...

1

2

(**2**) ...to make a blintz base. Turn the model over.

(**3**) Valley fold in the four corners...

3

(**4**) ...to a blintz base again. Turn the model over once more.

4

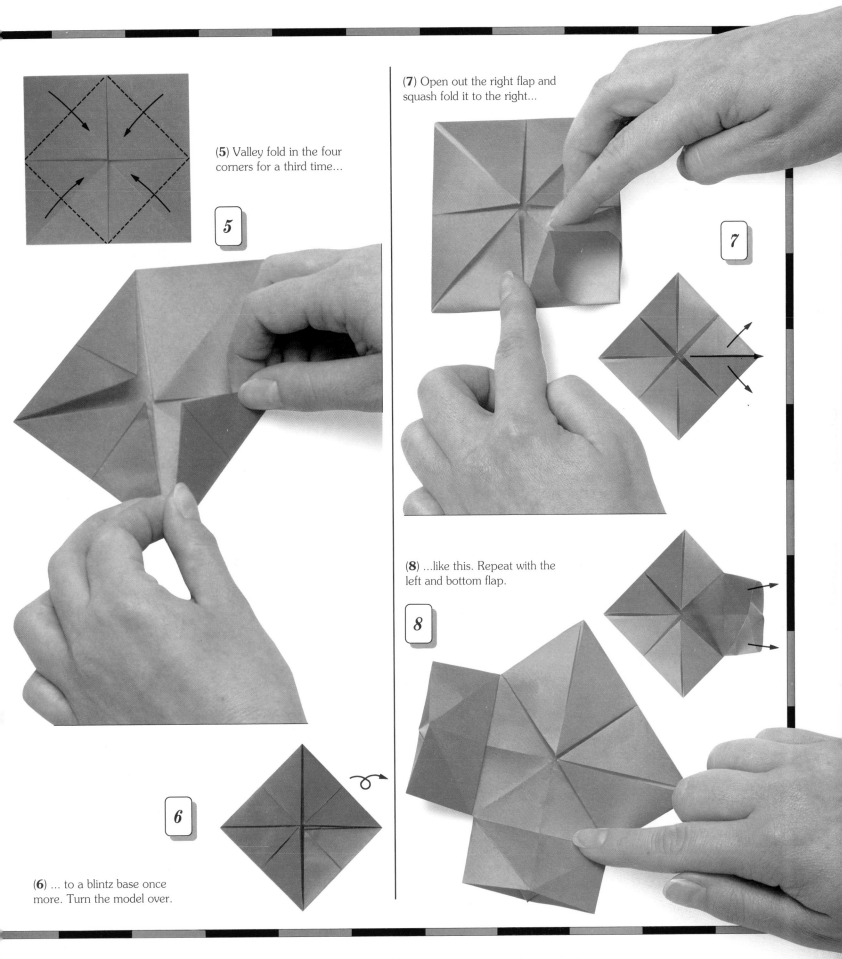

(**5**) Valley fold in the four corners for a third time...

5

(**6**) ... to a blintz base once more. Turn the model over.

6

(**7**) Open out the right flap and squash fold it to the right...

7

(**8**) ...like this. Repeat with the left and bottom flap.

8

9

(**9**) When you have done this, Yakko-San is completed.

(**10**) You can manufacture a whole string of Yakko-Sans and, by tucking one sleeve inside the other and fixing with a little glue, you will fashion a colourful crown or a cake decoration.

10

(**11**) and (**12**) are two variations of the Yakko-San fold which can be used on their own for chain decorations, or alternated with conventional Yakko-Sans for extra variety.

11

(**11**) Just squash fold the left and right sleeves to create this new form.

12

(**12**) In this variation *all four* sides are flattened. This version makes a most attractive napkin fold for your table.

THE HOUSE

Specially printed papers are sometimes produced in Japan for making this model. They show windows, furniture, plants, trees and people in an apparent haphazard jumble. When the model is folded, however, everything falls correctly into place in a delightful way. Start with a square.

1

(**1**) Fold and unfold the paper to create a centre guide line. Valley fold the top and bottom edges to meet this line.

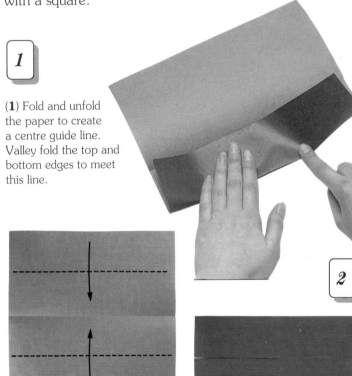

2

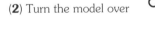
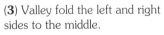

(**2**) Turn the model over

(**3**) Valley fold the left and right sides to the middle.

3

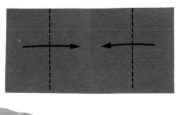

(**4**) Pull the top squares outwards, applying pressure with your fingers where shown...

4

5

(**5**) ...and squash fold them down into their new position. Turn the model over.

6 A

(**6**) Decorate your completed House with patches of coloured paper to represent the doors and windows. The effect can be quite realistic.

6 B

THE YACHT

This is one of the simplest folds imaginable and yet the finished result is very pleasing – especially if you use a square with contrasting colours on either side. The current trend in origami is "back to basics" – people are trying to achieve the maximum *effect* with the minimum number of folds. The yacht requires only *three*!

3

(**3**) Mountain fold the bottom section of the hull so that the Yacht will stand up

1

(**1**) Valley fold across the diagonal centre line, bringing the top point to the bottom.

4

(**2**) Outside reverse fold the hull.

2

(**4**) There you have it – simplicity itself!

KIMONO

A Kimono is a long, loose-fitting, Japanese outer garment with wide sleeves. We western folk have adopted this design in our dressing gowns and bath robes. Start with a length of paper of 3 x 1 proportions, e.g. 18 cm x 6 cm.

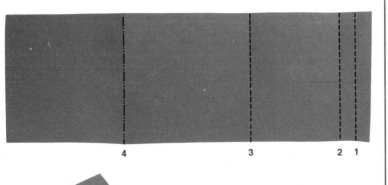

4   3   2   1

(**1**) Make the folds marked 1, 2, 3 and 4 in sequence. Folds 3 and 4 divide the strip into equal thirds. You may find it easier to measure and mark where these two folds should appear, because it is important that they are in the correct place. Folds 1, 2 and 3 are valley folds. Fold 4 is a mountain fold.

(**2**) Valley fold these two corners down at right angles to reach the centre line.

1 A

1 B

2 A

2 B

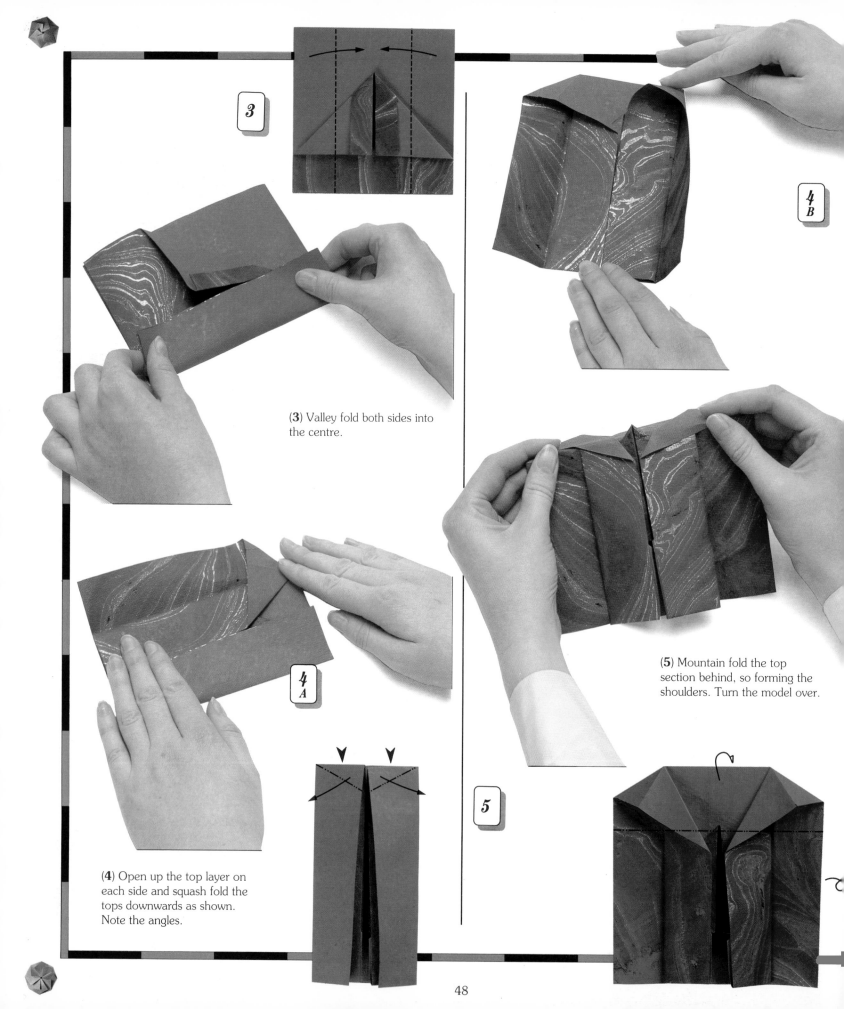

3

4 B

(3) Valley fold both sides into the centre.

(5) Mountain fold the top section behind, so forming the shoulders. Turn the model over.

4 A

5

(4) Open up the top layer on each side and squash fold the tops downwards as shown. Note the angles.

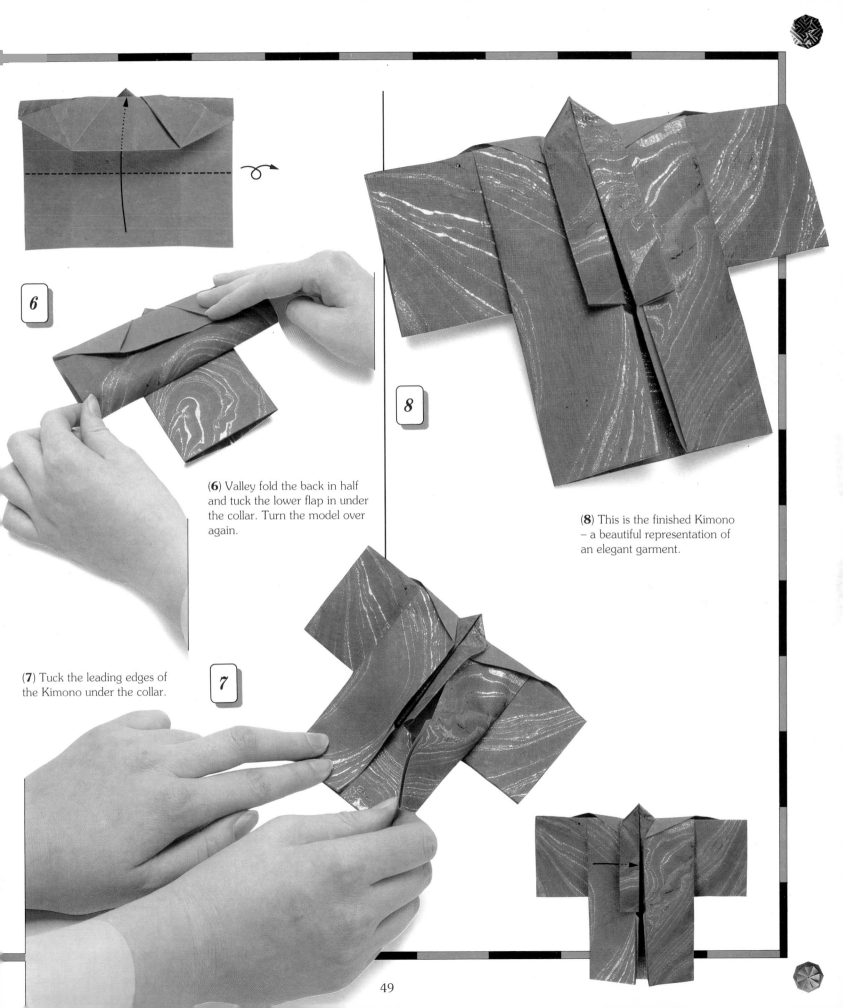

6

(**6**) Valley fold the back in half and tuck the lower flap in under the collar. Turn the model over again.

8

(**8**) This is the finished Kimono – a beautiful representation of an elegant garment.

(**7**) Tuck the leading edges of the Kimono under the collar.

7

THE CUP

If you fold this from a square of greaseproof paper you can make a practical paper cup from which you can drink. If you ever get marooned on a desert island, this origami fold could prove invaluable! Use a square of paper.

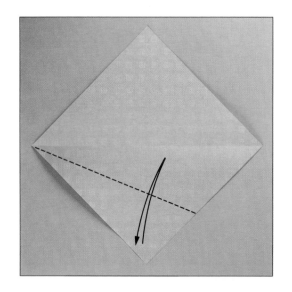

1

(**1**) Pre-crease the diagonal. Valley fold and then unfold the bottom side to the centre line.

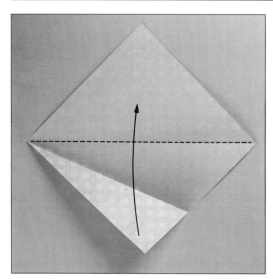

2

(**2**) Valley fold the square in half along the pre-creased diagonal.

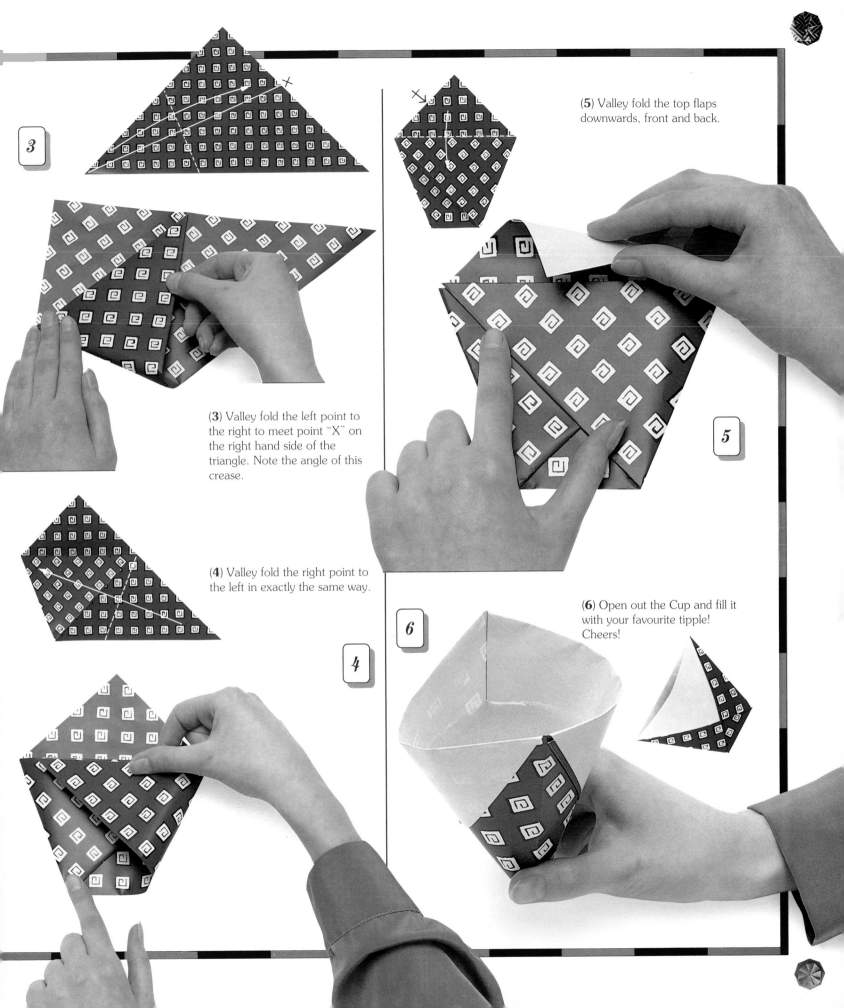

3

(**3**) Valley fold the left point to the right to meet point "X" on the right hand side of the triangle. Note the angle of this crease.

(**4**) Valley fold the right point to the left in exactly the same way.

4

(**5**) Valley fold the top flaps downwards, front and back.

5

(**6**) Open out the Cup and fill it with your favourite tipple! Cheers!

6

SAMPAN

This is one of the most beautiful folds in the whole realm of origami. The final opening-out sequence and revelation of the Sampan (a small boat much used in Japan and China) is quite remarkable. What sort of mind could have invented it? Was it arrived at by accident? The truth is lost in time, but the resulting model is a little miracle. Use a fairly large square piece of paper.

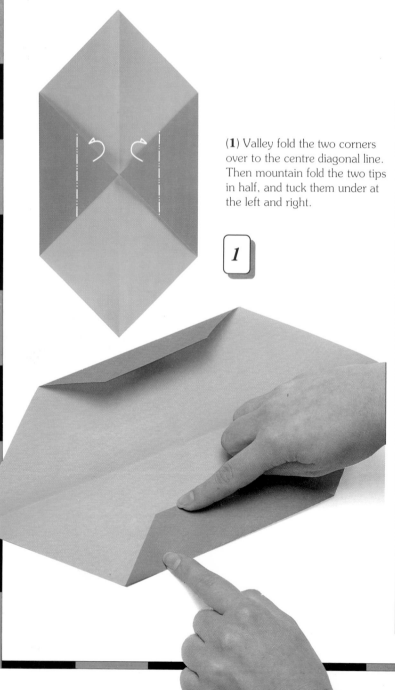

(**1**) Valley fold the two corners over to the centre diagonal line. Then mountain fold the two tips in half, and tuck them under at the left and right.

1

(**2**) Turn the model over.

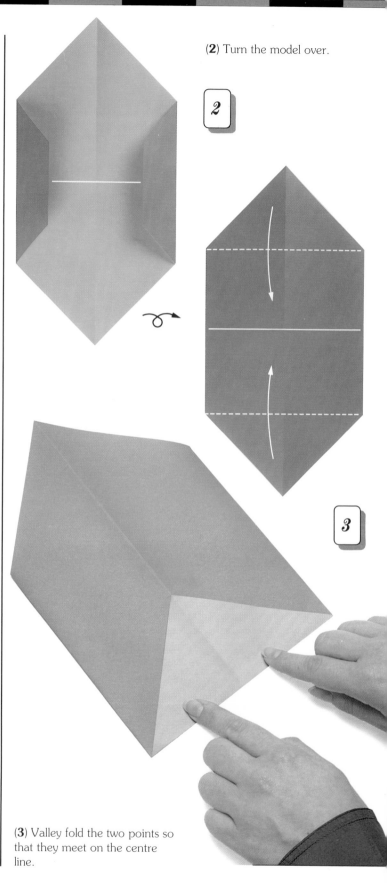

2

3

(**3**) Valley fold the two points so that they meet on the centre line.

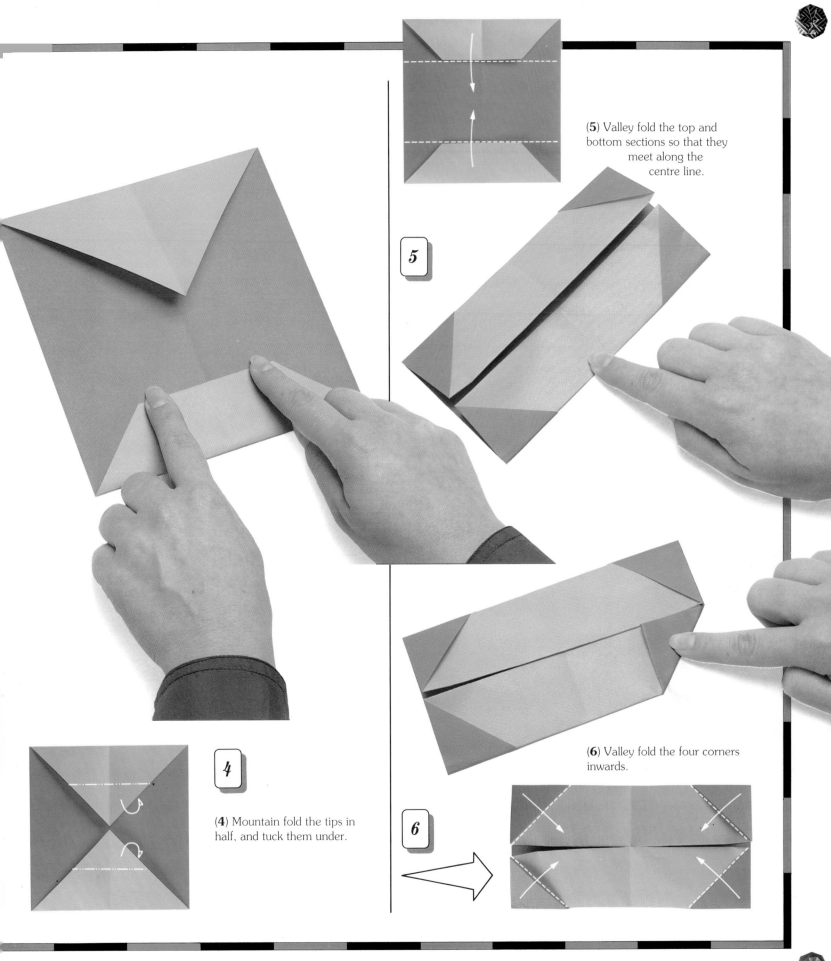

(**5**) Valley fold the top and bottom sections so that they meet along the centre line.

5

(**4**) Mountain fold the tips in half, and tuck them under.

4

(**6**) Valley fold the four corners inwards.

6

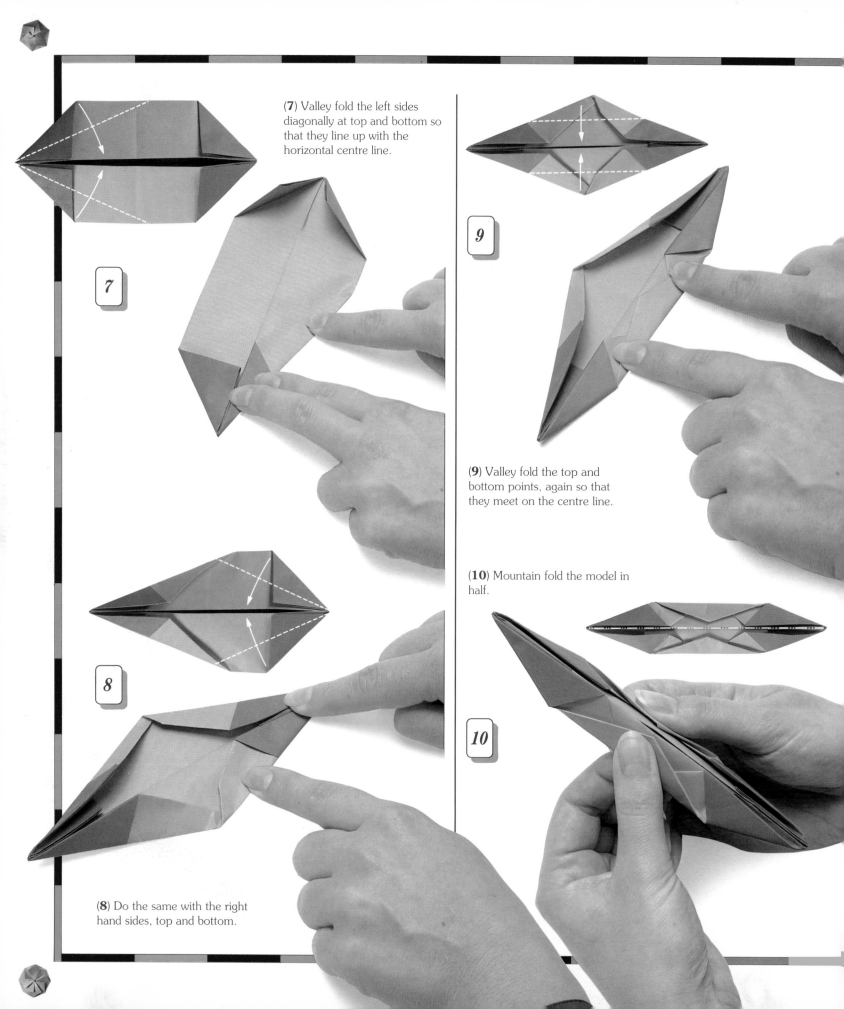

(**7**) Valley fold the left sides diagonally at top and bottom so that they line up with the horizontal centre line.

7

(**8**) Do the same with the right hand sides, top and bottom.

8

9

(**9**) Valley fold the top and bottom points, again so that they meet on the centre line.

(**10**) Mountain fold the model in half.

10

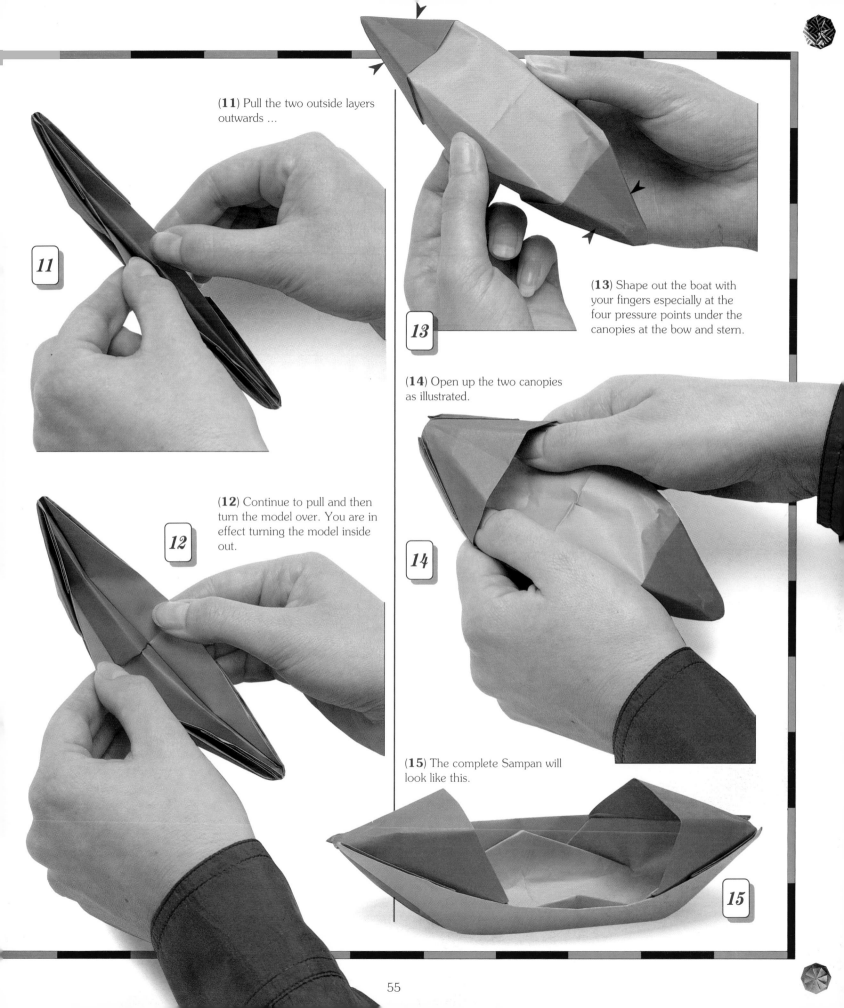

(**11**) Pull the two outside layers outwards ...

(**12**) Continue to pull and then turn the model over. You are in effect turning the model inside out.

(**13**) Shape out the boat with your fingers especially at the four pressure points under the canopies at the bow and stern.

(**14**) Open up the two canopies as illustrated.

(**15**) The complete Sampan will look like this.

BELT AND BUCKLE

I love this fold! It is very satisfying to do. The illusion at the end of a separate Belt and Buckle is quite remarkable. Folds (**13**) and (**14**) literally took my breath away when Robert Harbin first showed them to me. Use a square of paper.

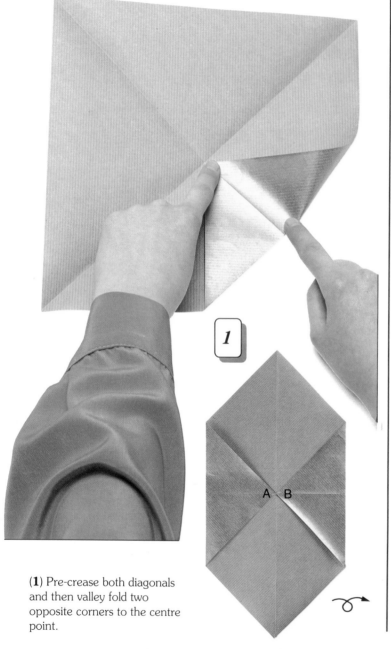

1

(**1**) Pre-crease both diagonals and then valley fold two opposite corners to the centre point.

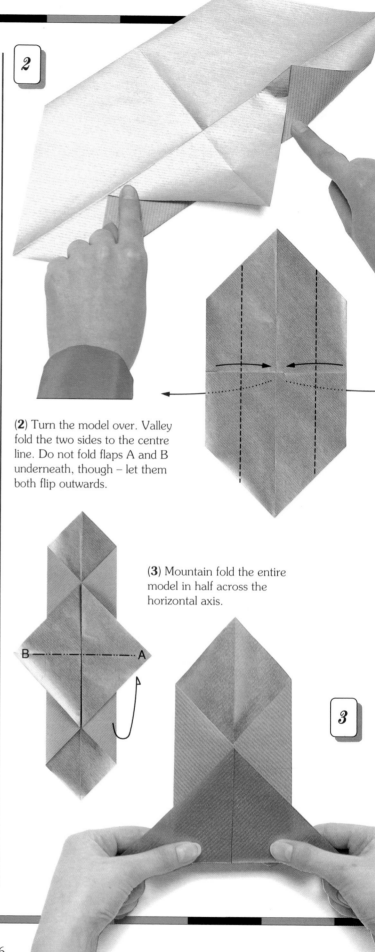

2

(**2**) Turn the model over. Valley fold the two sides to the centre line. Do not fold flaps A and B underneath, though – let them both flip outwards.

(**3**) Mountain fold the entire model in half across the horizontal axis.

3

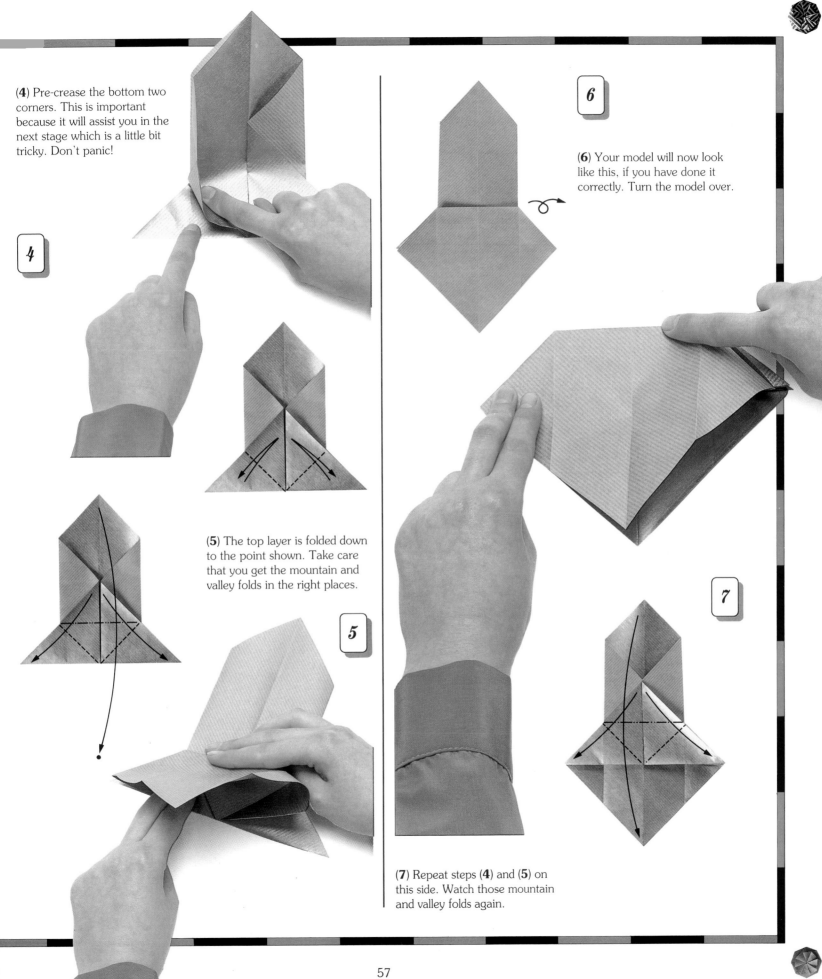

(**4**) Pre-crease the bottom two corners. This is important because it will assist you in the next stage which is a little bit tricky. Don't panic!

4

(**5**) The top layer is folded down to the point shown. Take care that you get the mountain and valley folds in the right places.

5

6

(**6**) Your model will now look like this, if you have done it correctly. Turn the model over.

7

(**7**) Repeat steps (**4**) and (**5**) on this side. Watch those mountain and valley folds again.

57

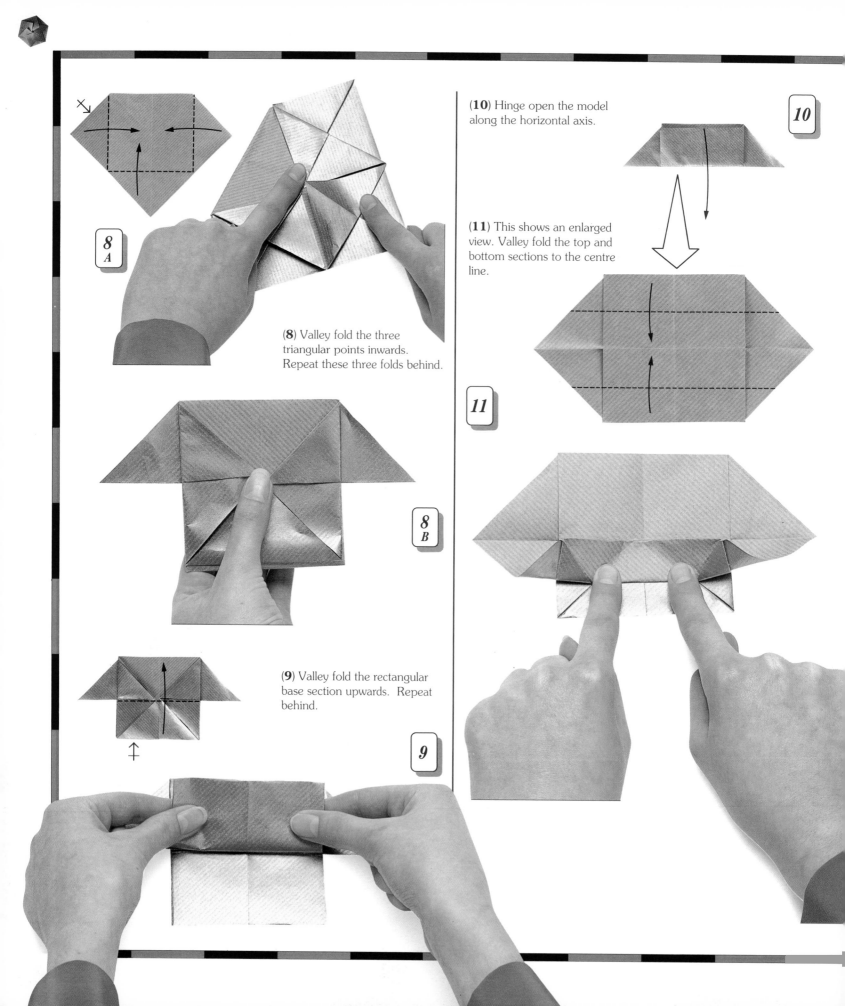

(**8**) Valley fold the three triangular points inwards. Repeat these three folds behind.

**8
A**

**8
B**

(**9**) Valley fold the rectangular base section upwards. Repeat behind.

9

(**10**) Hinge open the model along the horizontal axis.

10

(**11**) This shows an enlarged view. Valley fold the top and bottom sections to the centre line.

11

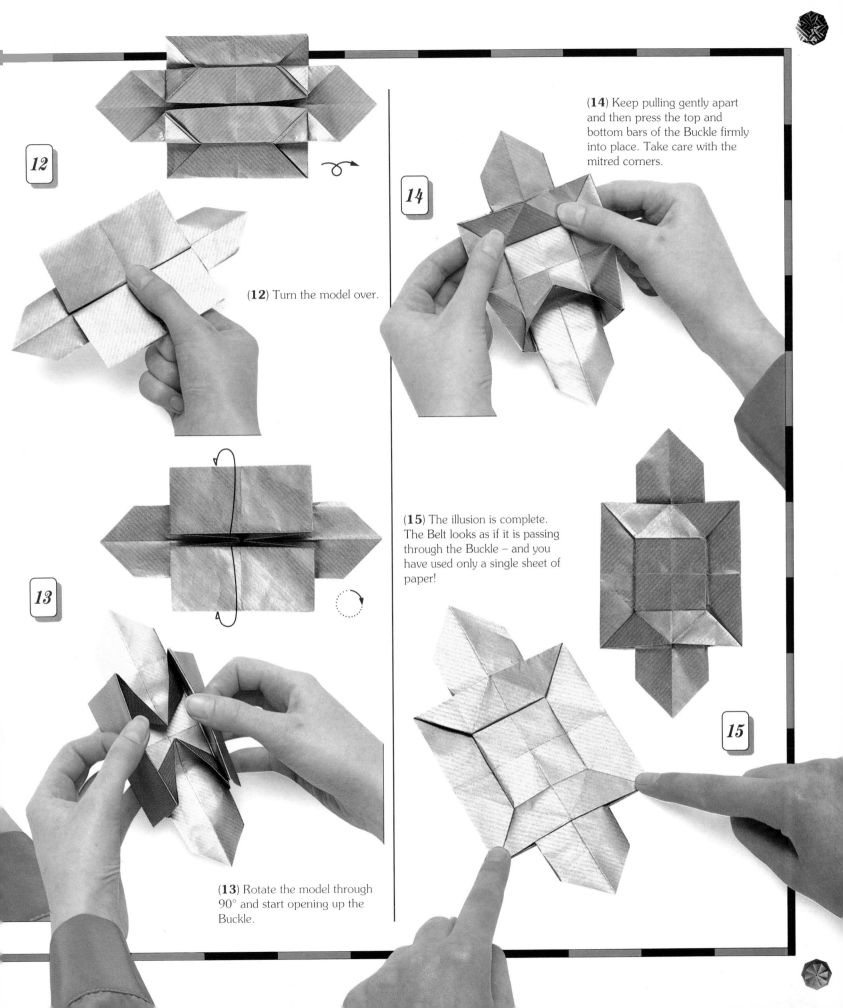

(12) Turn the model over.

(13) Rotate the model through 90° and start opening up the Buckle.

(14) Keep pulling gently apart and then press the top and bottom bars of the Buckle firmly into place. Take care with the mitred corners.

(15) The illusion is complete. The Belt looks as if it is passing through the Buckle – and you have used only a single sheet of paper!

THE JUNK

Life is full of surprises. So is origami! We have just folded a Belt and Buckle. We will now proceed from that to a Japanese Junk. By that, I do not mean the odds and ends that you find in a Japanese bric-à-brac shop – I refer to the beautiful boat that is found throughout the Far East.

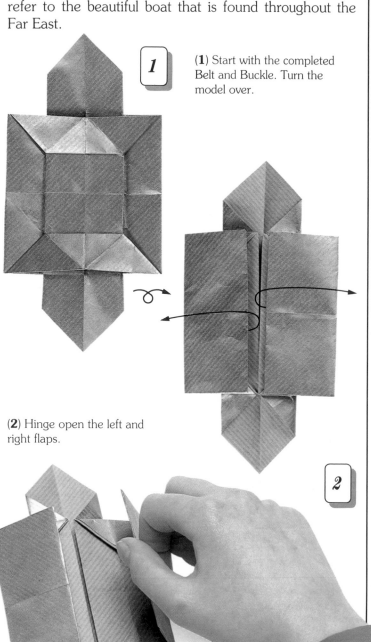

1 (**1**) Start with the completed Belt and Buckle. Turn the model over.

(**2**) Hinge open the left and right flaps.

2

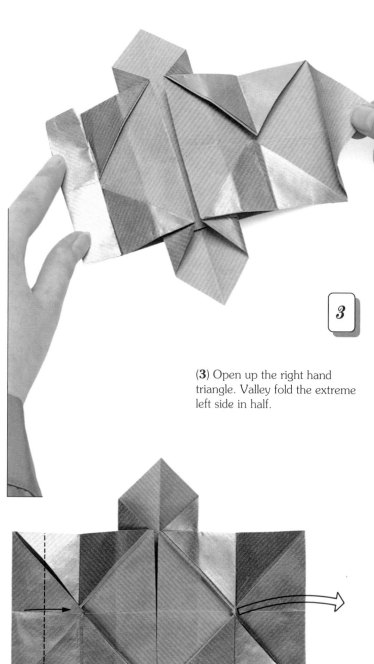

3

(**3**) Open up the right hand triangle. Valley fold the extreme left side in half.

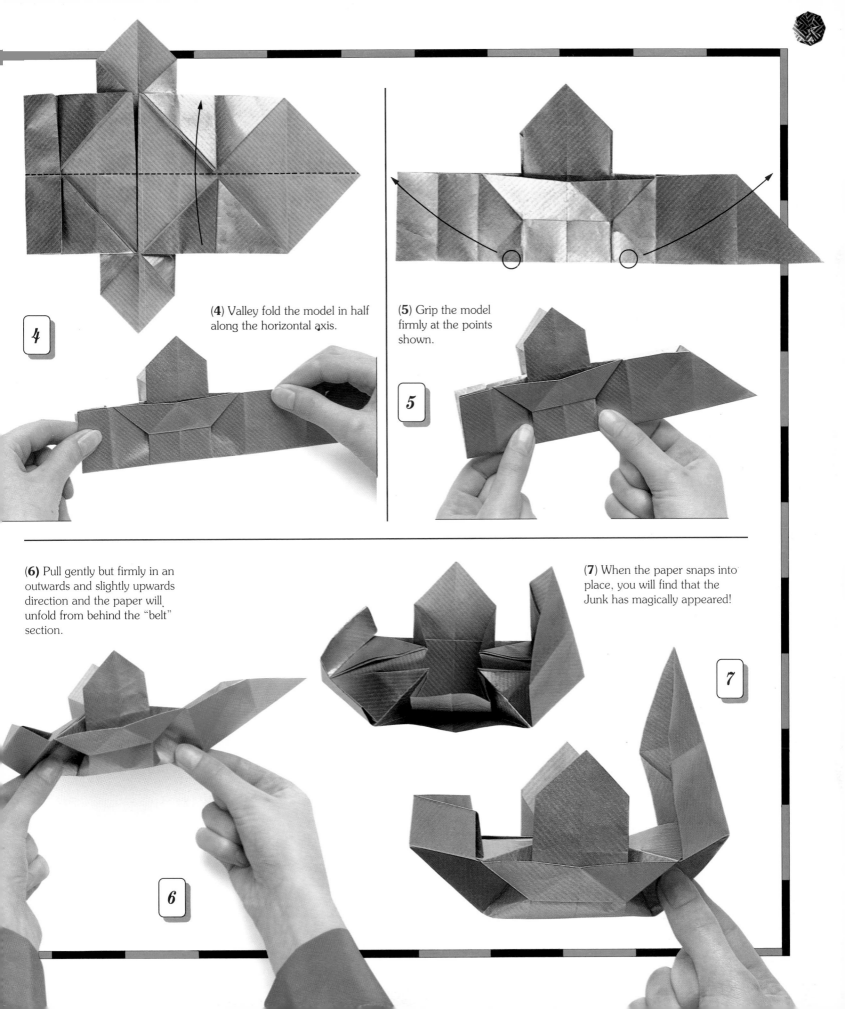

(**4**) Valley fold the model in half along the horizontal axis.

(**5**) Grip the model firmly at the points shown.

(**6**) Pull gently but firmly in an outwards and slightly upwards direction and the paper will unfold from behind the "belt" section.

(**7**) When the paper snaps into place, you will find that the Junk has magically appeared!

RED SAILS

While in a cruising mood, I want to introduce you to a cute traditional twin-sailed yacht. If you are lucky enough to holiday in Barbados, you may well see the "Jolly Roger" pirate boat that does excursions around the island. It resembles this simple, yet effective, classical fold. Use a square of paper, red on one side only.

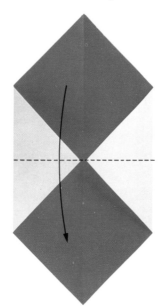

1

(**1**) The square should be positioned red side up. Pre-crease the diagonal. Fold the left and right points to the centre point. Valley fold the model in half across the horizontal axis.

(**2**) Lift the right half into an upright position and squash fold it down, following the valley and mountain folds indicated.

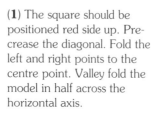

2

3

(**3**) Turn the model over.

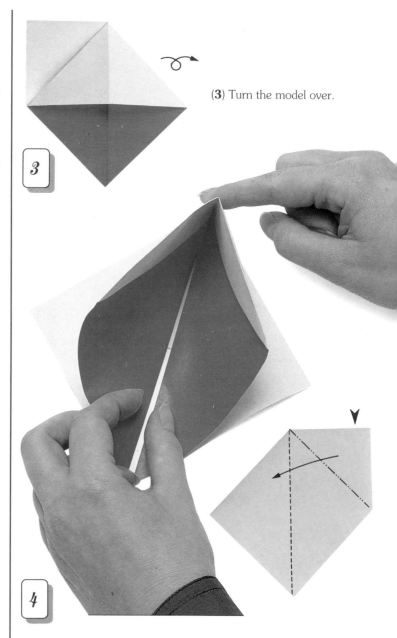

4

(**4**) Squash fold the other half in exactly the same way as (**2**).

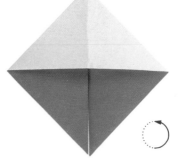

(**5**) Rotate the model through 180°.

5

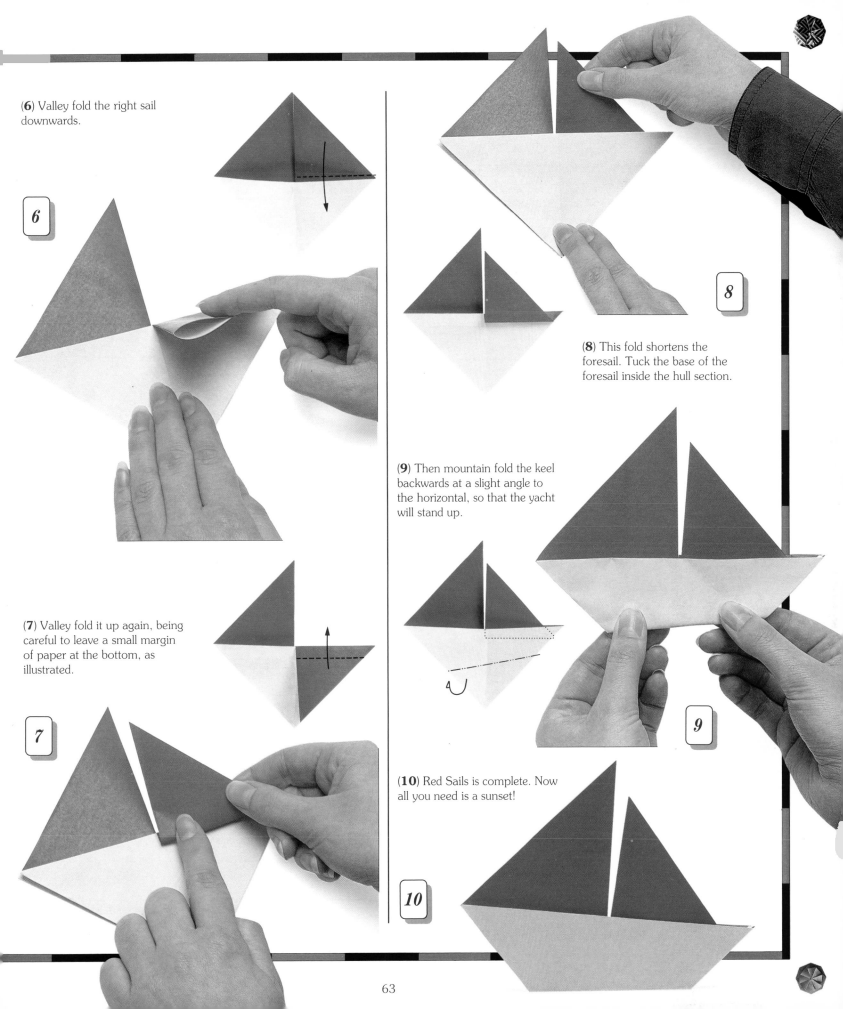

(**6**) Valley fold the right sail downwards.

6

(**7**) Valley fold it up again, being careful to leave a small margin of paper at the bottom, as illustrated.

7

(**8**) This fold shortens the foresail. Tuck the base of the foresail inside the hull section.

8

(**9**) Then mountain fold the keel backwards at a slight angle to the horizontal, so that the yacht will stand up.

9

(**10**) Red Sails is complete. Now all you need is a sunset!

10

THE WINDSURFER

Windsurfing is now extremely popular, but is of very recent invention. It was really only first developed in California in the late 1960s. This origami fold pre-dates the water sport by several centuries! It is a great favourite with young children. Use a square of paper.

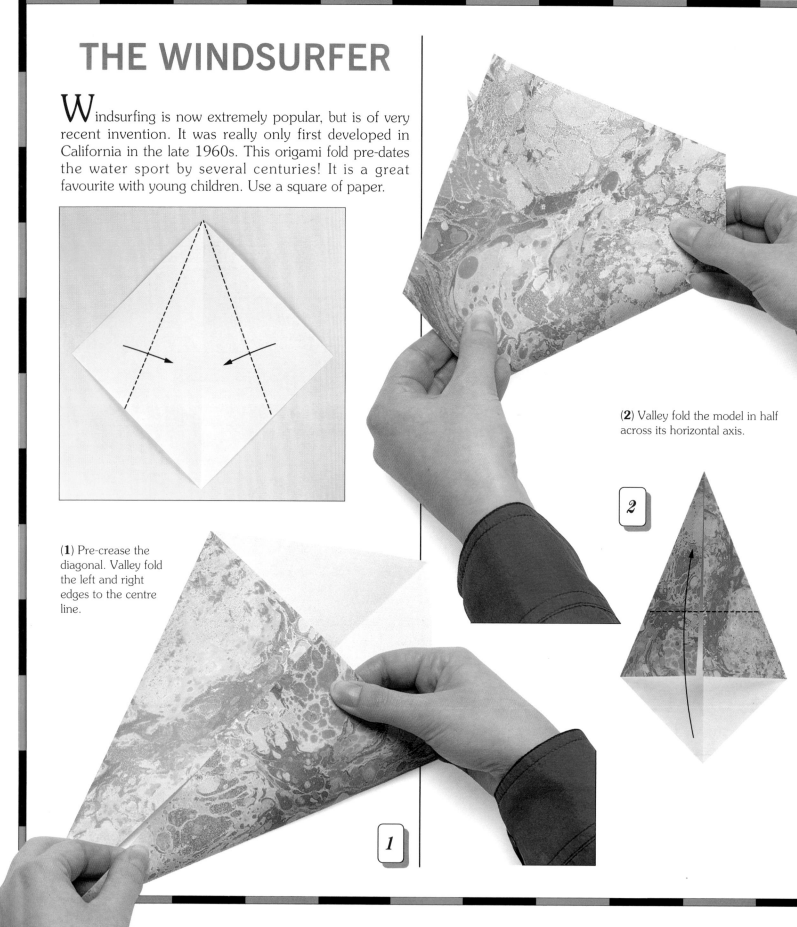

(**1**) Pre-crease the diagonal. Valley fold the left and right edges to the centre line.

(**2**) Valley fold the model in half across its horizontal axis.

(**3**) Valley fold the left and right sides to the centre.

3

(**4**) Valley fold the sail backwards into an upright position.

4

(**5**) Run the tip of the board section between your finger and thumb a few times, so that it curls upwards slightly.

5

6

(**6**) Launch the model and blow on the sail. The Windsurfer will skid across the surface of the water or a polished tabletop at great speed.

THE WATER BOMB

Many of our models have used a water bomb base. So, what is a Water Bomb? Follow these instructions and you will find out! Water Bombs make very attractive festive ornaments with which to decorate your Christmas tree. Children, when they are feeling evil, love to fill their Bombs with water and throw them at each other! Use a square of paper. Start with a water bomb base.

(**1**) Valley fold the left and right corners upwards to the centre line. so their tips meet at the apex of the triangle.

(**2**) Mountain fold the other two corners behind.

(**3**) Valley fold the left and right hand points to the centre line.

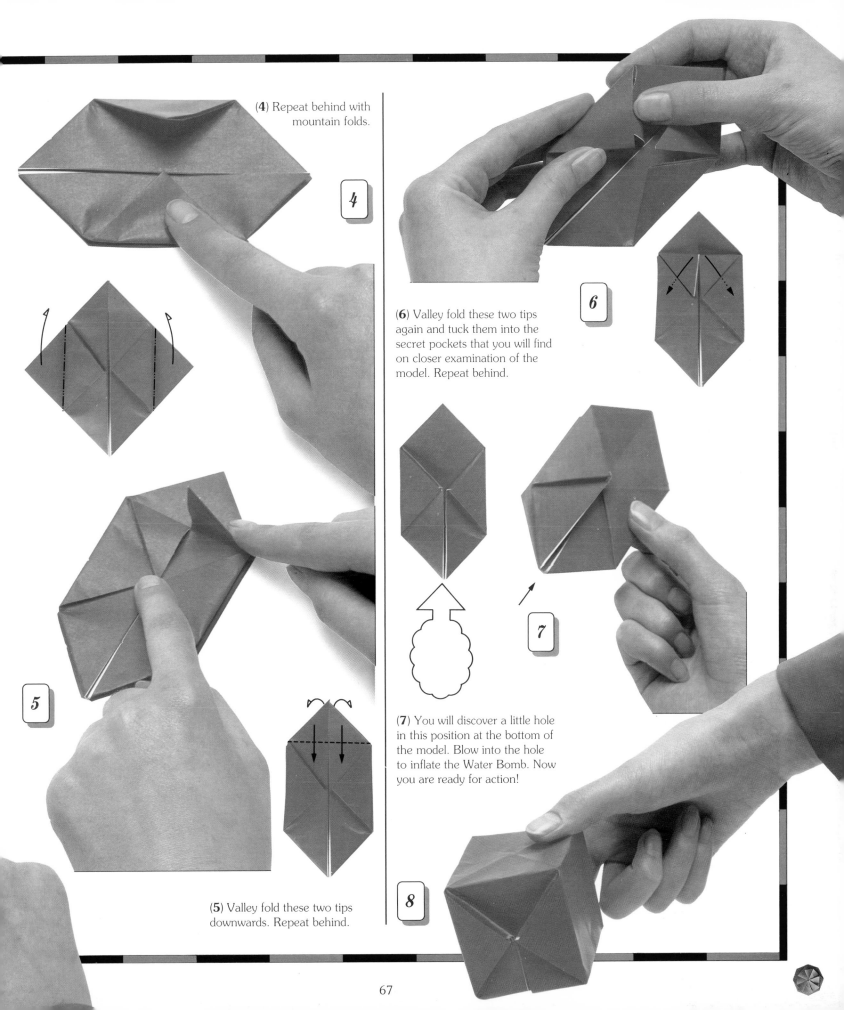

(**4**) Repeat behind with mountain folds.

4

(**5**) Valley fold these two tips downwards. Repeat behind.

5

(**6**) Valley fold these two tips again and tuck them into the secret pockets that you will find on closer examination of the model. Repeat behind.

6

(**7**) You will discover a little hole in this position at the bottom of the model. Blow into the hole to inflate the Water Bomb. Now you are ready for action!

7

8

THE PAGODA

A pagoda is a kind of temple or sacred building found in the Far East; it consists of a pyramidal tower several storeys high. This impressive model is made from five squares of paper. These are of varying sizes, e.g. 6cm, 7cm, 8cm, 9cm and 10cm respectively. They can either be the same colour or five different colours depending upon your personal preference. All five are folded in the same way and at the end are nested one on top of the other to form the Pagoda. Start with a water bomb base.

(1) Valley fold the bottom left and right corners to the centre line. Repeat behind.

1

2

(2) Lift each flap into an upright position. Open them up one by one, and squash fold them downwards to form square shapes. Repeat behind.

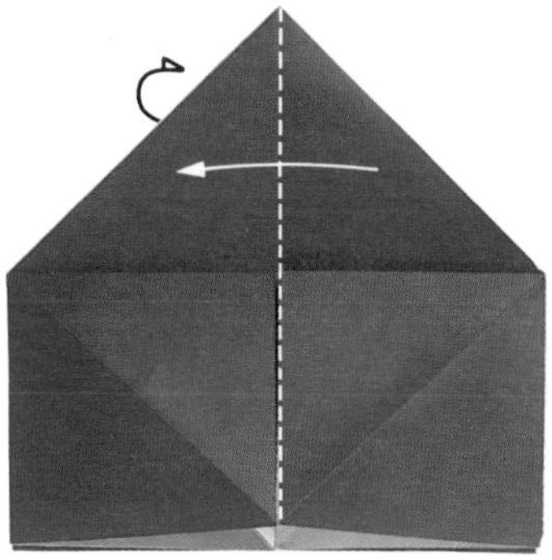

(**3**) Valley fold the right side of the model to the left. Repeat behind.

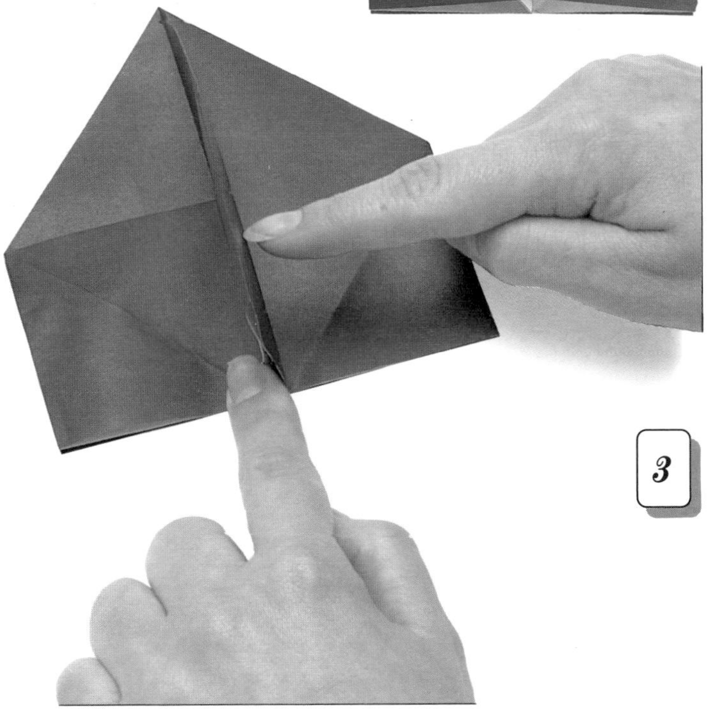

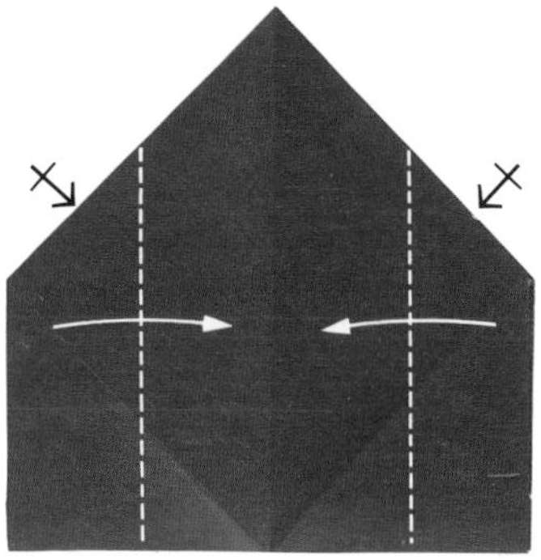

(**4**) Valley fold the left and right sides inwards to the centre line. Repeat behind.

3

4

5

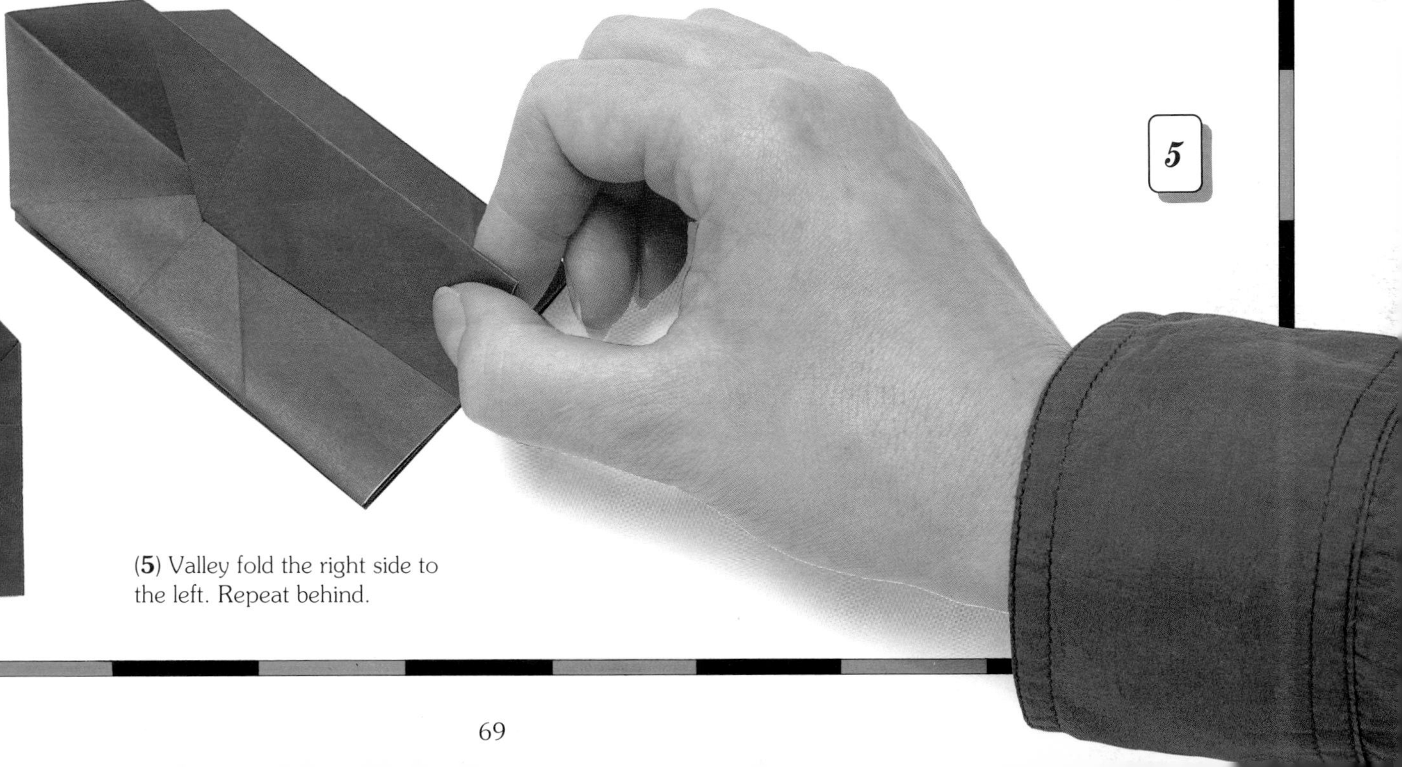

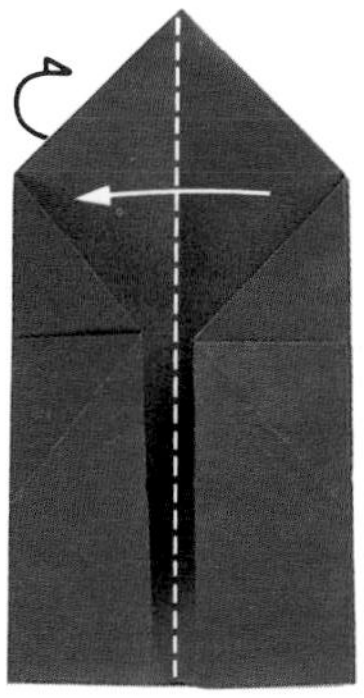

(**5**) Valley fold the right side to the left. Repeat behind.

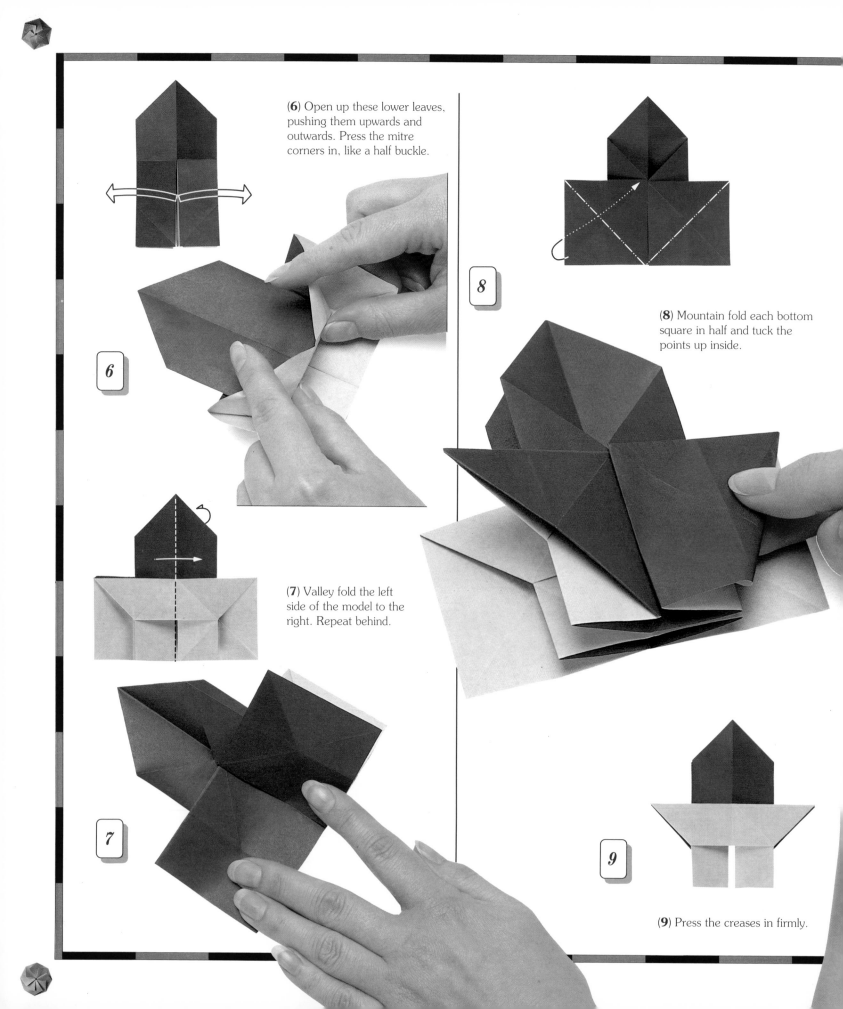

(**6**) Open up these lower leaves, pushing them upwards and outwards. Press the mitre corners in, like a half buckle.

(**7**) Valley fold the left side of the model to the right. Repeat behind.

(**8**) Mountain fold each bottom square in half and tuck the points up inside.

(**9**) Press the creases in firmly.

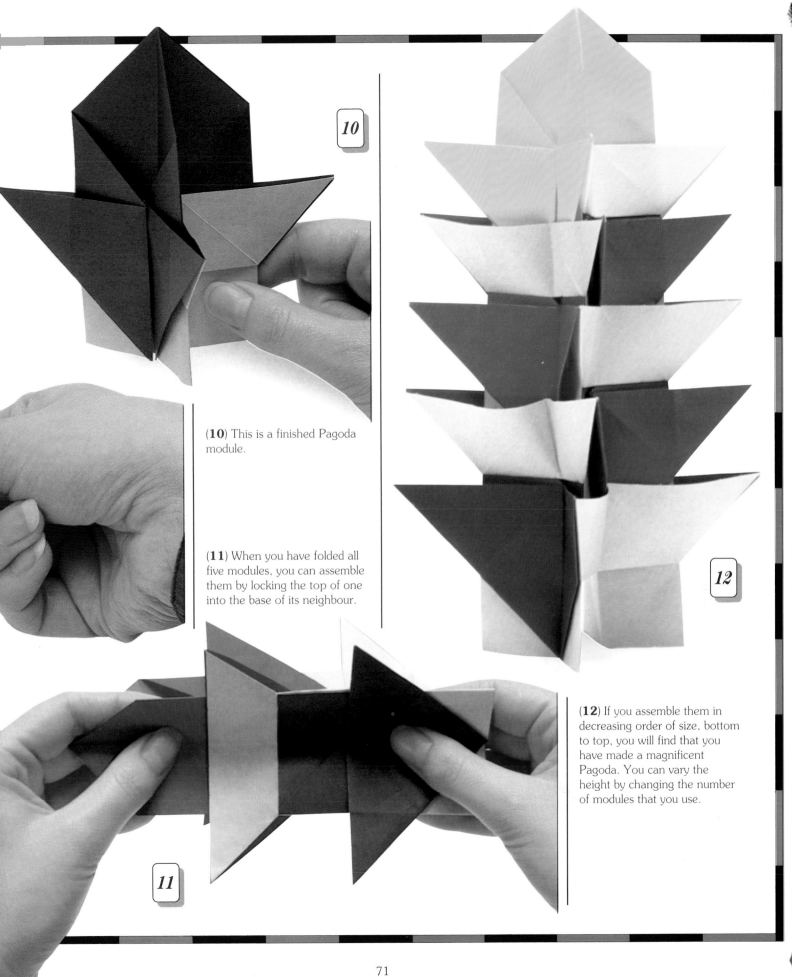

(**10**) This is a finished Pagoda module.

(**11**) When you have folded all five modules, you can assemble them by locking the top of one into the base of its neighbour.

(**12**) If you assemble them in decreasing order of size, bottom to top, you will find that you have made a magnificent Pagoda. You can vary the height by changing the number of modules that you use.

THE CUBE

Modular origami is very popular among modern day folders who nowadays are keen to create many beautiful interlocking models. This is a traditional Japanese interlocking model – which just goes to show that there is nothing new under the sun! Use six squares of paper. Fold each one as explained below.

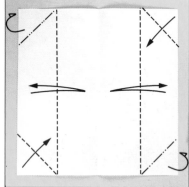

(**1**) Pre-crease the vertical centre line. Valley fold the left and right sides to this centre line and unfold them again. Mountain fold the top left and bottom right corners. Valley fold the top right and bottom left corners.

(**2**) Valley fold both sides to the centre.

(**3**) Valley fold the bottom right corner and tuck it under the left side.

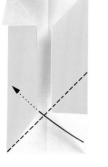

(**4**) Valley fold the top left corner and tuck it under the right hand side flap.

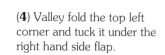

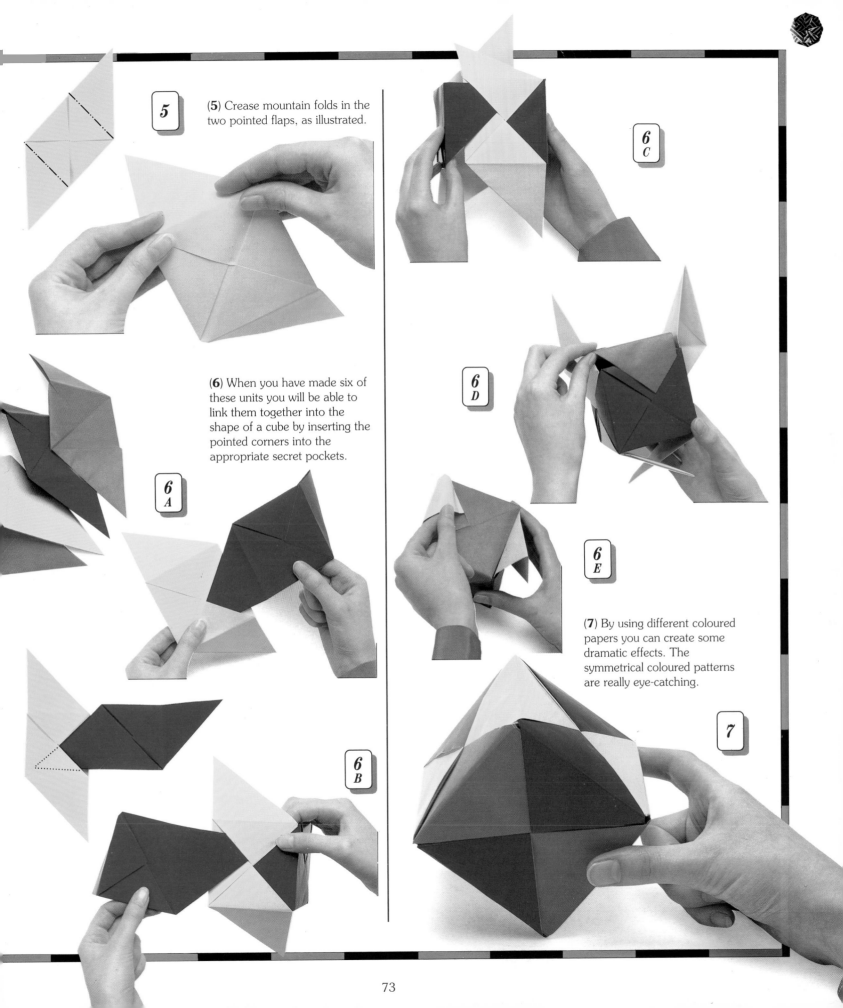

5 (5) Crease mountain folds in the two pointed flaps, as illustrated.

(6) When you have made six of these units you will be able to link them together into the shape of a cube by inserting the pointed corners into the appropriate secret pockets.

6 A

6 B

6 C

6 D

6 E

(7) By using different coloured papers you can create some dramatic effects. The symmetrical coloured patterns are really eye-catching.

7

ANIMAL MAGIC

GNASHERS

This simple action model is very popular with children. The jaws are strong enough to pick up a small object or a piece of paper. I use it to help me perform card tricks. Gnashers finds the chosen card and picks it out of the pack between his teeth. Use an A4 sheet of paper.

(**1**) Valley fold the paper in half from top to bottom.

(**2**) Valley fold the front flap upwards. Repeat behind.

(**3**) Mountain fold the corners – tucking them behind. In this case, fold back three thicknesses of paper. Repeat behind with the remaining one thickness of paper.

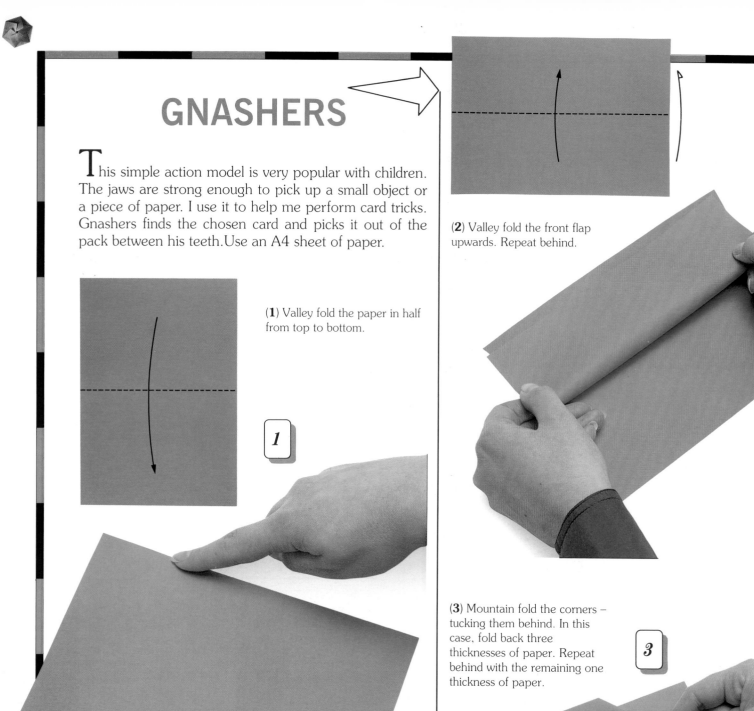

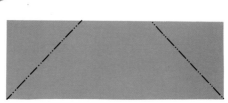

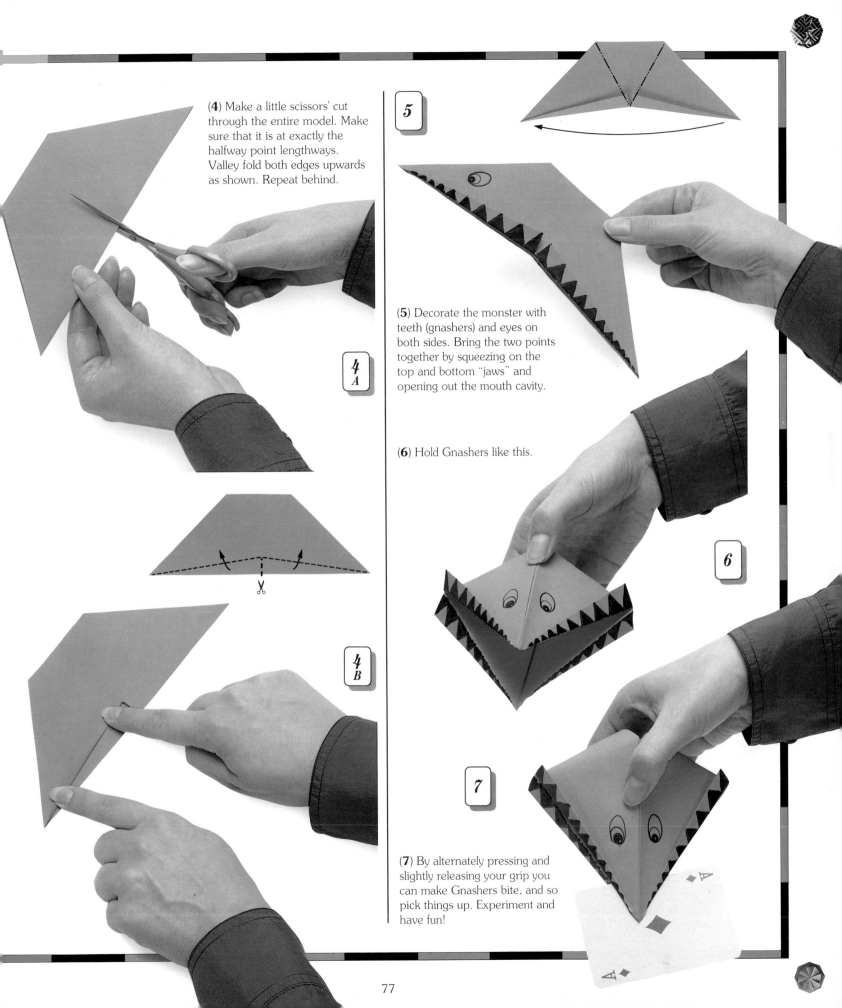

(**4**) Make a little scissors' cut through the entire model. Make sure that it is at exactly the halfway point lengthways. Valley fold both edges upwards as shown. Repeat behind.

4 A

4 B

5

(**5**) Decorate the monster with teeth (gnashers) and eyes on both sides. Bring the two points together by squeezing on the top and bottom "jaws" and opening out the mouth cavity.

(**6**) Hold Gnashers like this.

6

7

(**7**) By alternately pressing and slightly releasing your grip you can make Gnashers bite, and so pick things up. Experiment and have fun!

THE BUTTERFLY

The butterfly is a very popular object for the origami practitioner. Many beautiful folds have been created of this graceful insect. Of particular beauty are the butterfly folds of Akira Yoshizawa. Robert Harbin taught me the following fold. He told me that it was Japanese in origin, but could not tell me who designed it. Whoever the creator was, I feel sure that he was greatly influenced by Akira Yoshizawa. Use a square of paper.

(**1**) Start with a water bomb base. Valley fold down both the flaps to the centre line.

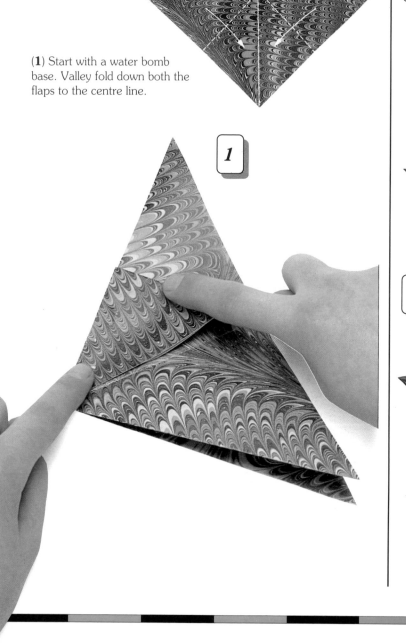

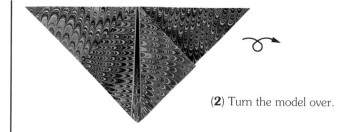

(**2**) Turn the model over.

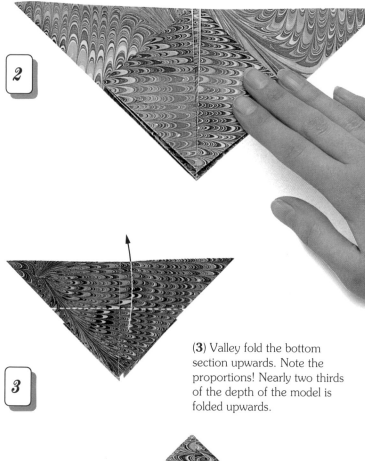

(**3**) Valley fold the bottom section upwards. Note the proportions! Nearly two thirds of the depth of the model is folded upwards.

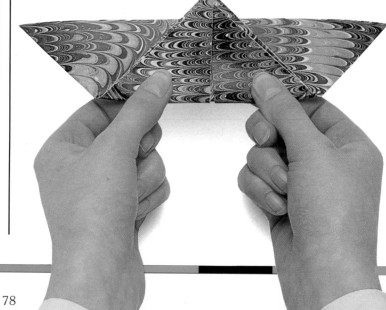

(**4**) Bring both front flaps down – push in at the edges where shown and press this section flat.

(**5**) The two folds at the head should be executed in order. The first is a mountain fold at the shoulder and the second a valley fold forwards. When you have done that, book fold the butterfly in half from left to right.

(**6**) Valley fold the wings downwards on both sides.

(**7**) Open out the model, and there you have an extremely beautiful Butterfly.

THE BLUEBIRD

This little bird is very easy to make. The scissors' cut creates his cuteness. It is a traditional Japanese fold, the origins of which are uncertain. I feel that it is very much in the style of Isao Honda. If this is the case, it would not be as old as we have been led to believe. Use a square that has a contrasting colour on each side. Given its name, blue is an ideal choice.

(1) Valley fold the two sides to the centre line. Mountain fold the top triangle behind.

1

(2) Valley fold the top left and right points downwards to the centre line.

2

(3) Lift the right flap into an upright position.

3

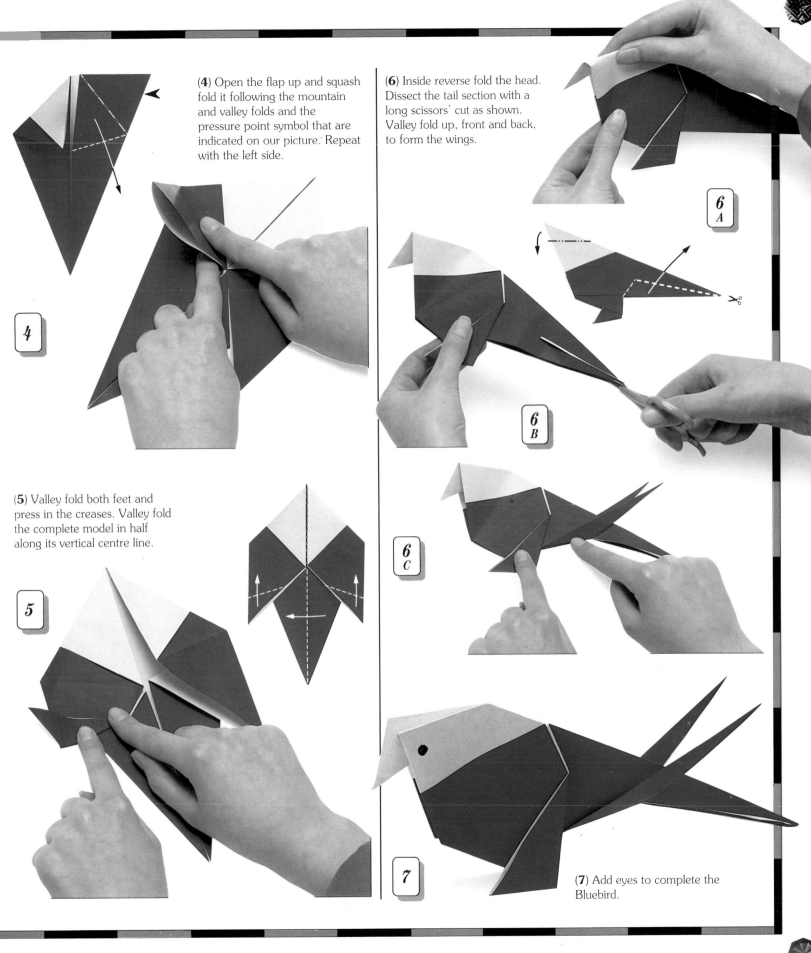

(4) Open the flap up and squash fold it following the mountain and valley folds and the pressure point symbol that are indicated on our picture. Repeat with the left side.

4

(5) Valley fold both feet and press in the creases. Valley fold the complete model in half along its vertical centre line.

5

(6) Inside reverse fold the head. Dissect the tail section with a long scissors' cut as shown. Valley fold up, front and back, to form the wings.

6 A

6 B

6 C

7

(7) Add eyes to complete the Bluebird.

PUPPY LOVE

For sheer simplicity this cute little Puppy is hard to beat. Only ten folds are used, and the result is an appealing creature that really has a character of its own. It is a two piece model – both squares should be of the same size and colour.

(**1**) Valley fold the square across the diagonal. Valley fold the bottom point which makes the nose upwards. Valley fold the two side corners that make the ears inwards. Take care to get the angles right.

THE HEAD

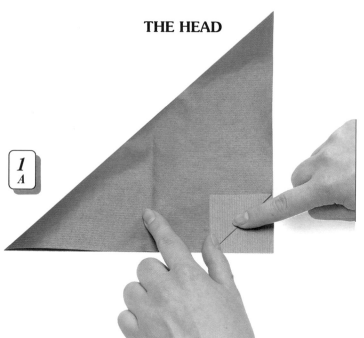

1 A

1 B

(**2**) Open up and squash fold the ears downwards applying pressure where shown.

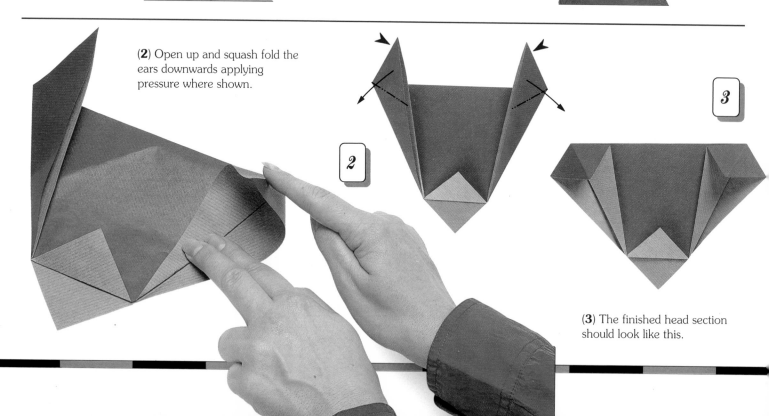

2

3

(**3**) The finished head section should look like this.

THE BODY

(**4**) Start with the square in the "diamond" position. Valley fold the left and right sides inwards. Note that they are *not* folded to meet on the centre line but run parallel to it. Make sure you leave a gap as shown. Mountain fold the lower triangular section behind, so that it is out of view.

(**5**) Mountain fold the top point behind. Sink the two lower corners with inside reverse folds.

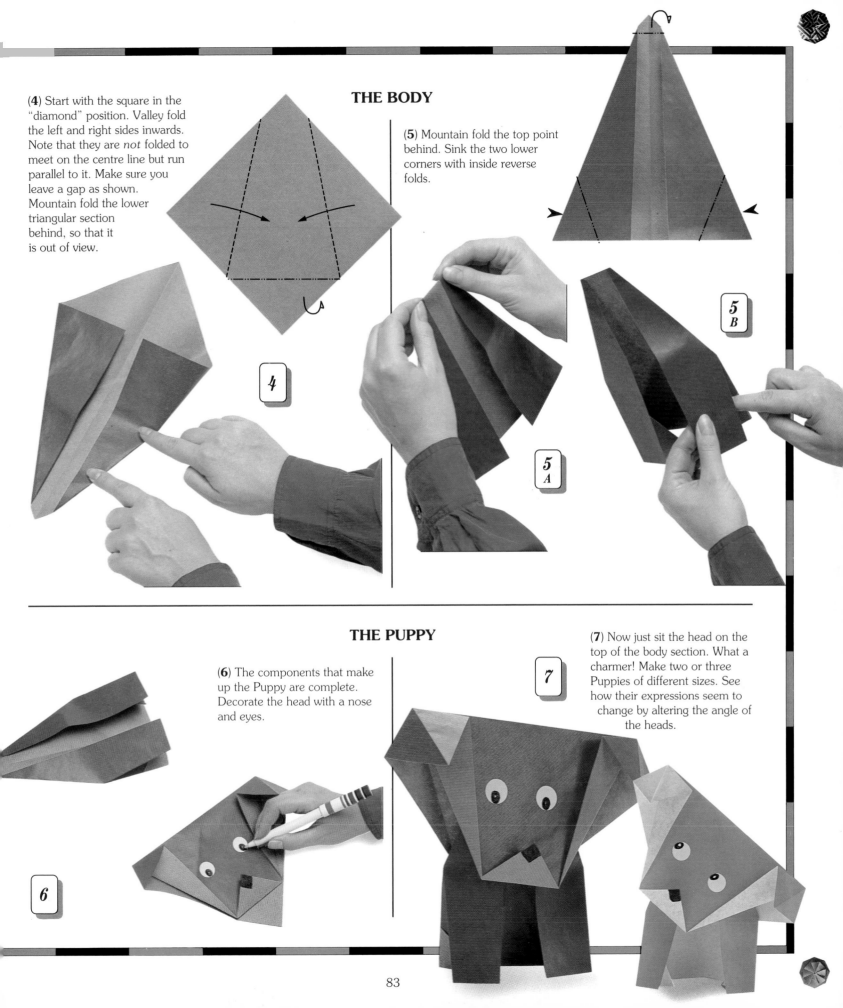

4

5
A

5
B

THE PUPPY

(**6**) The components that make up the Puppy are complete. Decorate the head with a nose and eyes.

(**7**) Now just sit the head on the top of the body section. What a charmer! Make two or three Puppies of different sizes. See how their expressions seem to change by altering the angle of the heads.

7

6

THE OWL

This beautiful model requires a couple of cuts but is all the better for them. It has appeared in other origami books, but is never credited to a specific creator. It is another example of a wonderful traditional fold that has been handed down through the generations. It is far too good to miss. Start with a square piece of paper (preferably brown and patterned to mimic a bird's plumage) and fold it into a bird base.

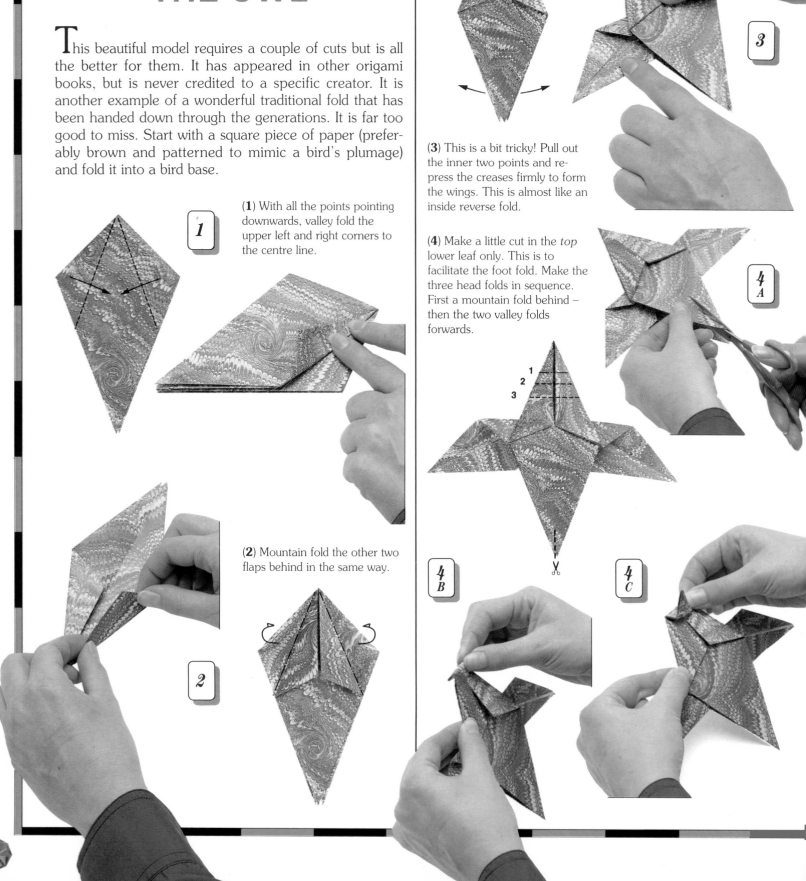

(**1**) With all the points pointing downwards, valley fold the upper left and right corners to the centre line.

(**2**) Mountain fold the other two flaps behind in the same way.

(**3**) This is a bit tricky! Pull out the inner two points and re-press the creases firmly to form the wings. This is almost like an inside reverse fold.

(**4**) Make a little cut in the *top* lower leaf only. This is to facilitate the foot fold. Make the three head folds in sequence. First a mountain fold behind – then the two valley folds forwards.

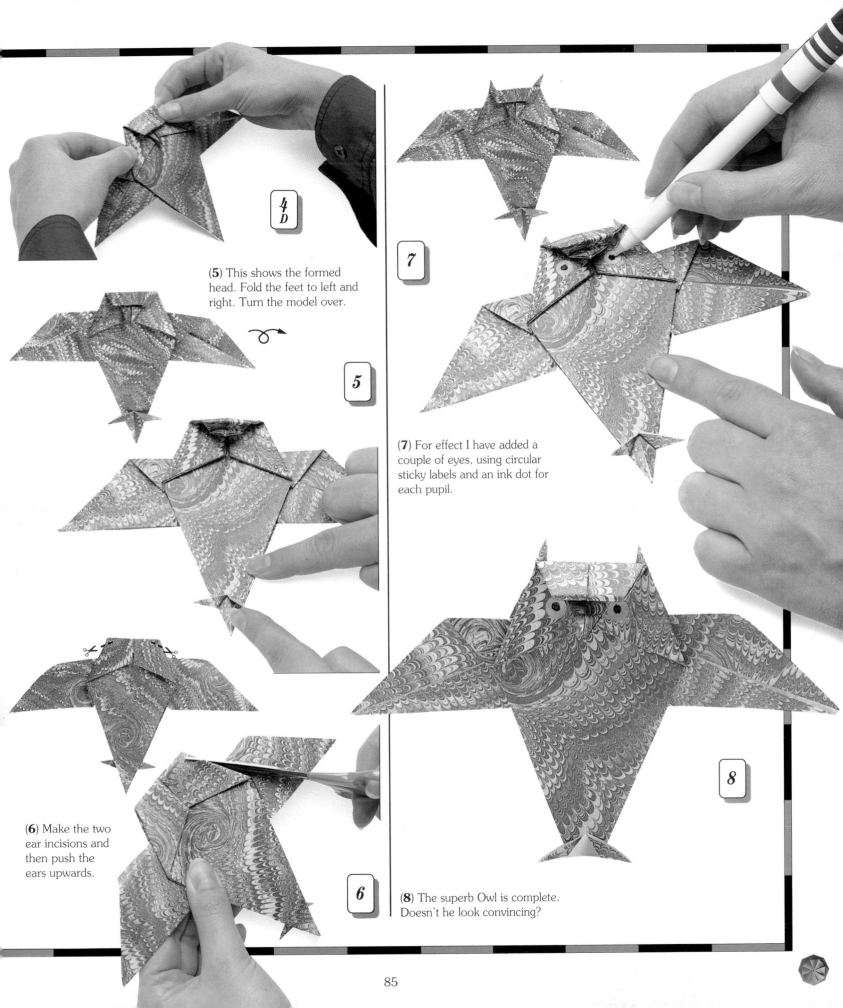

(**5**) This shows the formed head. Fold the feet to left and right. Turn the model over.

(**6**) Make the two ear incisions and then push the ears upwards.

(**7**) For effect I have added a couple of eyes, using circular sticky labels and an ink dot for each pupil.

(**8**) The superb Owl is complete. Doesn't he look convincing?

THE RABBIT

This traditional Japanese design "suggests" rather than "depicts" this lovable creature. The Japanese are absolute masters of the art of simplicity – knowing when to stop is part of the secret of a classic design. I love its uncluttered simplicity. Use a square of coloured paper.

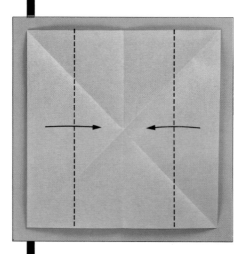

(1) Prepare by valley folding both diagonals and valley folding the vertical centre line. Open up the sheet again.

1

(2) Valley fold in the left and right edges to the vertical centre line.

2

(3) Valley fold the top half of the model to the centre point.

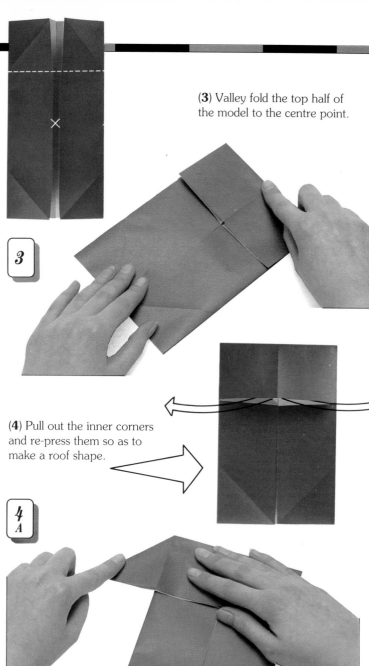

3

(4) Pull out the inner corners and re-press them so as to make a roof shape.

4 A

4 B

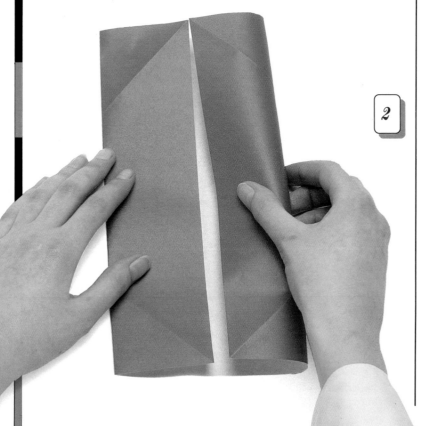

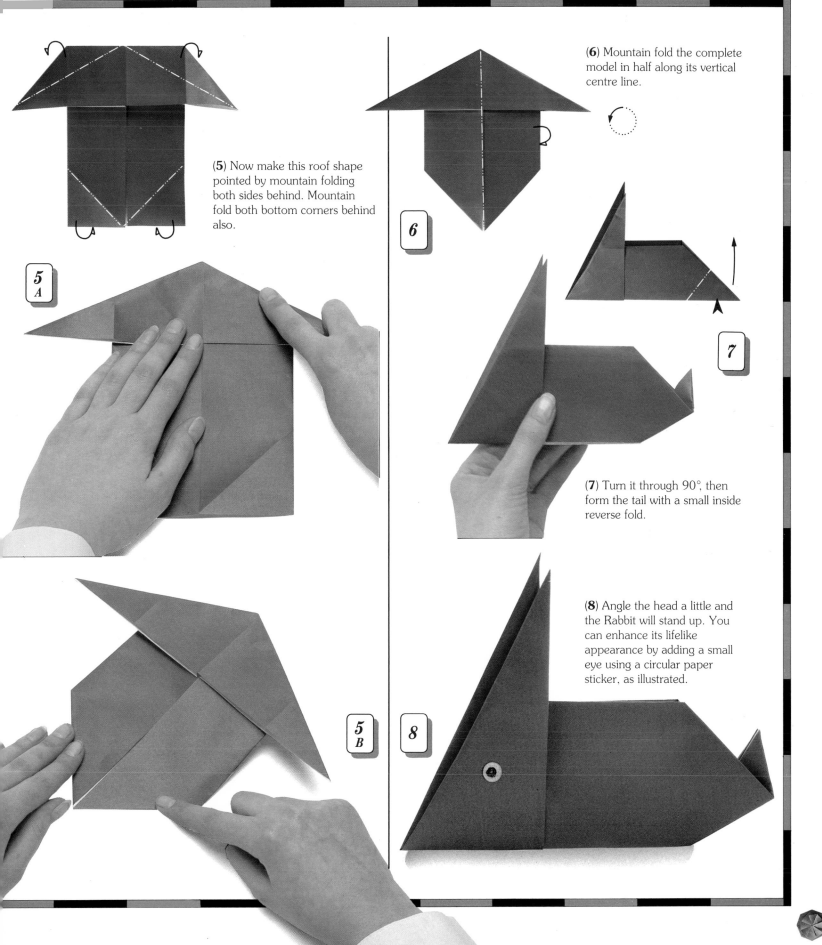

(**5**) Now make this roof shape pointed by mountain folding both sides behind. Mountain fold both bottom corners behind also.

5 A

5 B

(**6**) Mountain fold the complete model in half along its vertical centre line.

6

7

(**7**) Turn it through 90°, then form the tail with a small inside reverse fold.

8

(**8**) Angle the head a little and the Rabbit will stand up. You can enhance its lifelike appearance by adding a small eye using a circular paper sticker, as illustrated.

A SYMBOLIC BIRD

(**2**) Valley fold the top left and bottom left sides to the centre line.

With just *five* folds, you transform a square of paper into a bird. As the design is quite stylized, it could be a swan, a duck, a nesting pigeon, any one of a hundred different species, but it is very definitely a bird. When you have acquired a little more folding skill, you will be able to add extra folds to this Symbolic Bird so that it takes on the specific characteristics of the particular bird that you wish to represent. Start with a square of paper.

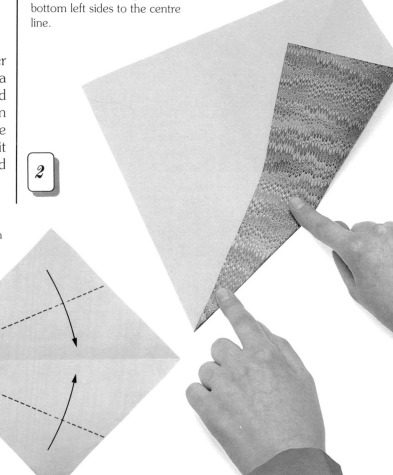

2

(**1**) Pre-crease the diagonal with a valley fold. Turn the paper over.

1

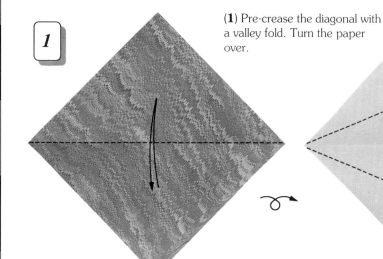

(**3**) Valley fold the left side to the right. Note where the point ends up.

3

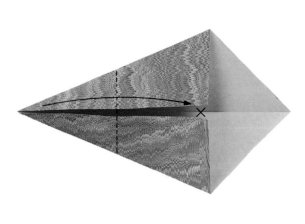

(**4**) Valley fold the triangle that makes the head back to the left.

4

5

(**5**) Mountain fold the complete bird in half down the horizontal centre line.

6

(**6**) Hold the model in the two places indicated and pull the neck and head into a more upright position.

7

(**7**) Crease the folds firmly so that the new position is maintained and your bird is complete. Simple, but very convincing.

THE FLAPPING BIRD

This is the most famous origami fold. It is also used in the logo of the British Origami Society. As I said in the introduction to this book, once you have folded a Flapping Bird, you will become totally hooked on origami. Fold one for a child and you will be his or her friend for life. Use a square of paper and start with a bird base.

(**1**) Valley fold the left side across to the right. Repeat behind.

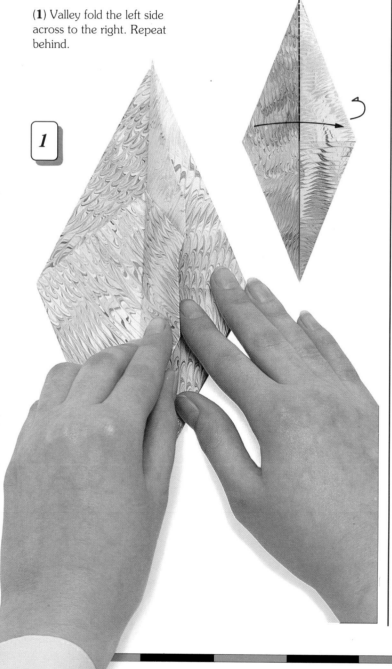

(**2**) Valley fold the sections that will form the wings upwards, front and back

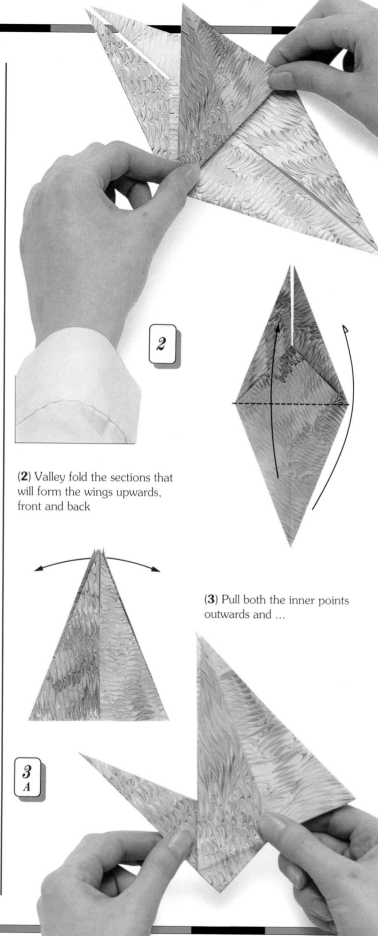

(**3**) Pull both the inner points outwards and ...

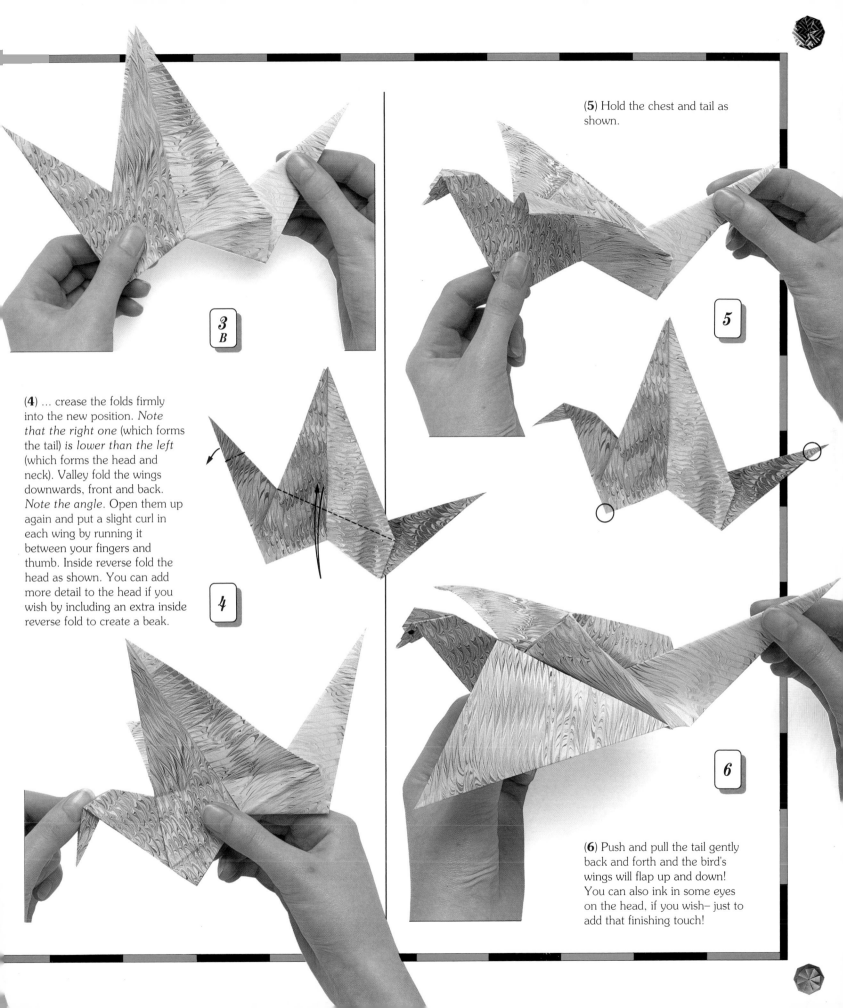

(5) Hold the chest and tail as shown.

3 B

(4) ... crease the folds firmly into the new position. *Note that the right one* (which forms the tail) *is lower than the left* (which forms the head and neck). Valley fold the wings downwards, front and back. *Note the angle.* Open them up again and put a slight curl in each wing by running it between your fingers and thumb. Inside reverse fold the head as shown. You can add more detail to the head if you wish by including an extra inside reverse fold to create a beak.

4

5

6

(6) Push and pull the tail gently back and forth and the bird's wings will flap up and down! You can also ink in some eyes on the head, if you wish– just to add that finishing touch!

THE CRANE

The Crane – a long-necked bird – was adopted as a symbol of good luck and long life by the Chinese Taoists. The most ancient Japanese origami books deal with methods of folding the bird, and in that country it is looked upon as a symbol of good luck. These days, the crane is to the Japanese what the dove is to us in the West: it is a symbol of peace.

The atomic bomb that was dropped on Hiroshima at the end of World War II made an orphan of a twelve-year-old girl called Sadako Sasaki. She was taken to hospital suffering from radiation sickness. She was appalled at what she had experienced and devastated as more children died in her hospital ward every day. She prayed for universal peace and, in the way of children, set herself the task of folding 1,000 cranes using the small squares of paper that her powdered medicine came in. She believed that if she achieved her aim of 1,000 cranes, her prayers would be answered. Sadly, she had completed only 644 before she became a victim of the terrible atomic radiation herself. In Hiroshima Park a statue was erected in her honour in 1958.

A thousand cranes strung together is called Sembazuru and it is said that if you manage to make one within any one year of your life you will have great fortune and longevity. Use a square of paper and start with a bird base.

(**1**) Valley fold the left and right sides of the diamond shape to the centre line. Repeat behind.

(**2**) Inside reverse fold both lower points upwards as far as they will go.

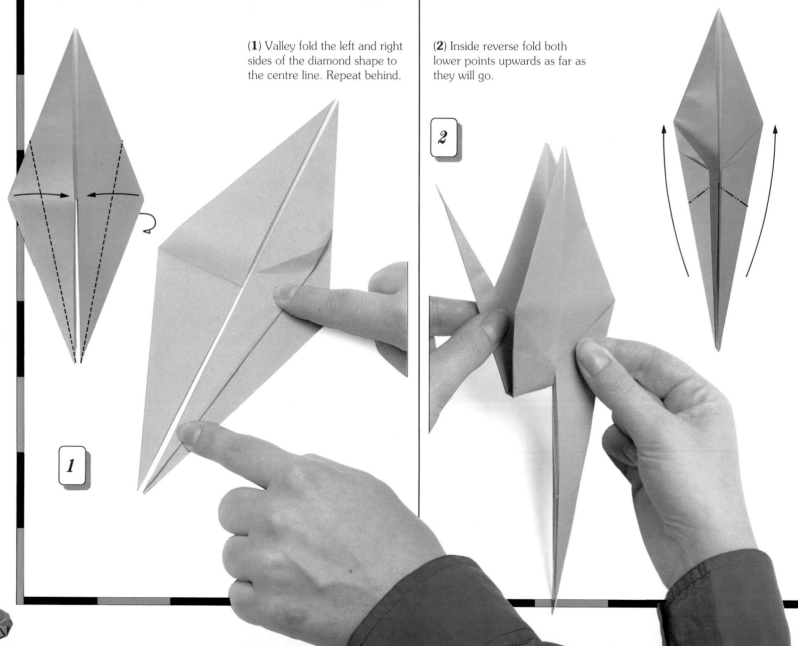

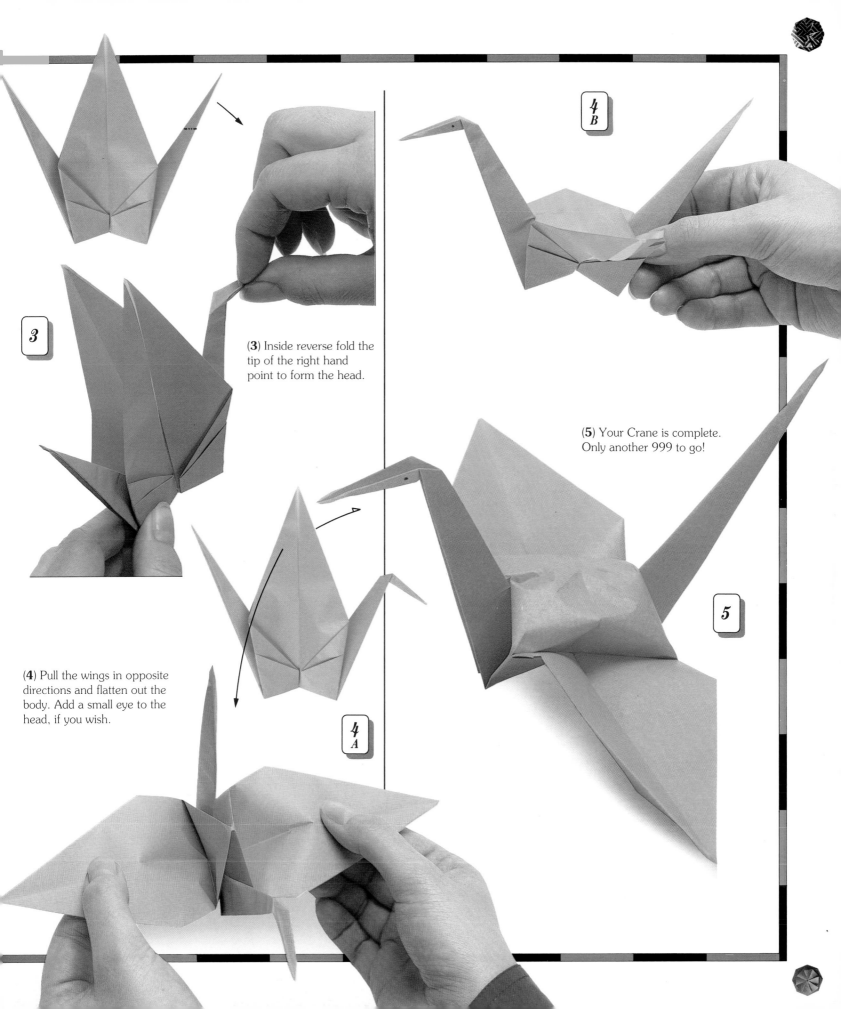

(**3**) Inside reverse fold the tip of the right hand point to form the head.

3

4 B

(**5**) Your Crane is complete. Only another 999 to go!

(**4**) Pull the wings in opposite directions and flatten out the body. Add a small eye to the head, if you wish.

4 A

5

THE CHIHUAHUA

I fiddle with bits of paper in the same way that some Middle Eastern gentlemen fiddle with worry beads! It is quite surprising what you can come up with while indulging in paper therapy! One afternoon, quite recently, I suddenly found that I was holding a little Chihuahua, the miniature Mexican hairless dog with large, pointed ears! I had to back-track and unfold the model in order to discover how, absent mindedly, I had arrived at it. Use a square of paper, either brown, grey or flesh coloured. Start with a water bomb base.

(**2**) Mountain fold the two resulting left and right hand points behind.

2

(**1**) Valley fold the left and right hand points upwards so that they meet at the apex of the triangle.

1

3

(**3**) Valley fold the tips downwards. Note the slight angle at which these folds should be made.

(4) Turn the model over.

(5) Valley fold the sides of the triangle to the centre line.

5

(6) Valley fold both sides upwards. Note the angles again.

6

(7) Again valley fold both sides upwards.

7

(8) Turn the model over.

8

9
A

(9) Mark large eyes on both sides of the head and the Chihuahua is finished. It is almost life-size!

9
B

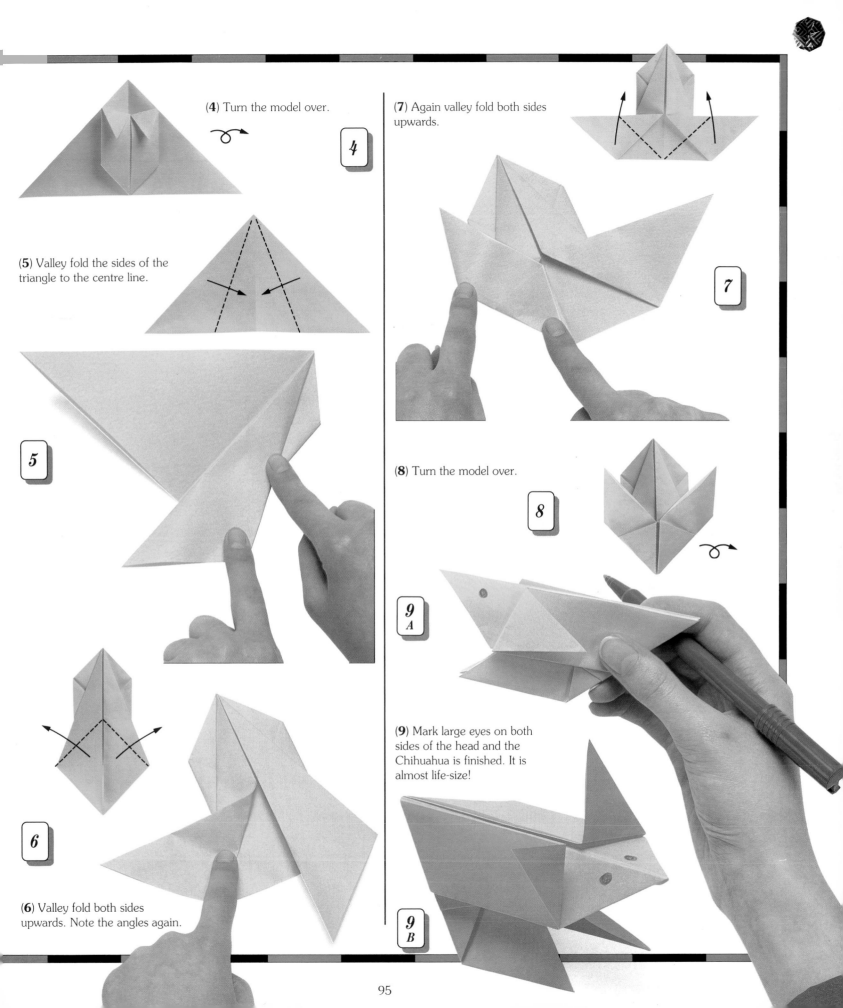

THE PEACOCK

Try to find a nice patterned paper when you make this model. I managed to find a green feathery design for the tail plumes, which is most effective. Always keep your eyes open for unusual paper that you may be able to use for your origami models. Alertness pays dividends! Use two square pieces of paper. Fold the first piece into a bird base, then work through the following steps.

(**1**) Inside reverse fold both bottom points outwards as far as shown. These will form the legs.

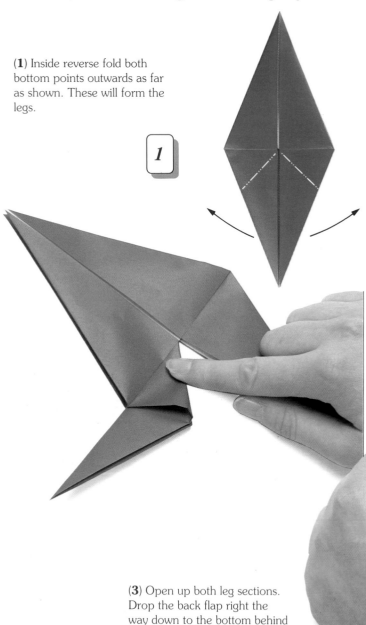

1

(**2**) Valley fold the top left and right sides inwards to the centre line.

2

3
A

(**3**) Open up both leg sections. Drop the back flap right the way down to the bottom behind the model.

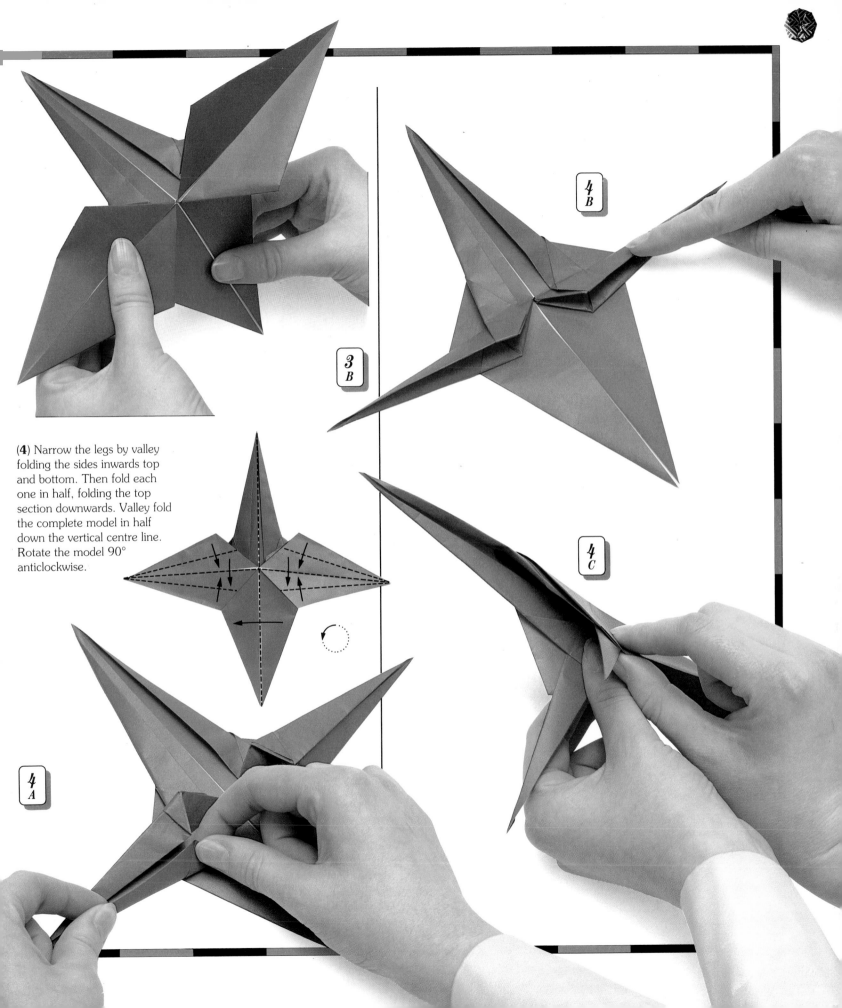

3
B

4
B

4
C

4
A

(**4**) Narrow the legs by valley folding the sides inwards top and bottom. Then fold each one in half, folding the top section downwards. Valley fold the complete model in half down the vertical centre line. Rotate the model 90° anticlockwise.

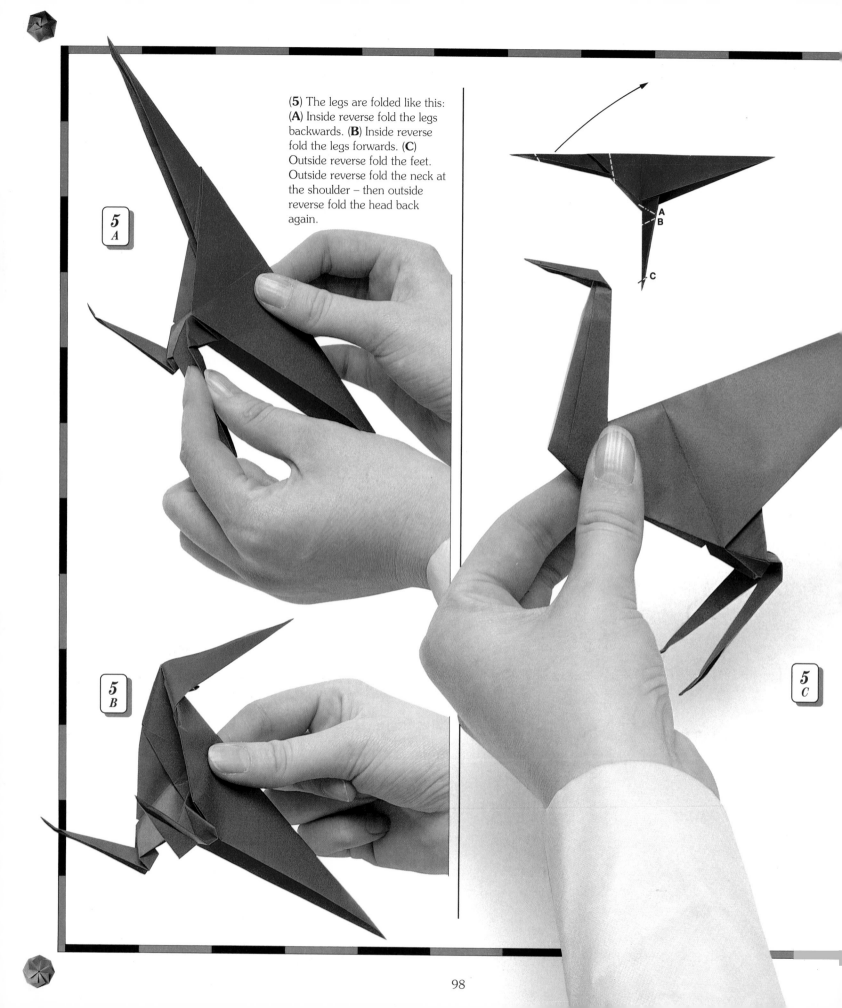

(**5**) The legs are folded like this: (**A**) Inside reverse fold the legs backwards. (**B**) Inside reverse fold the legs forwards. (**C**) Outside reverse fold the feet. Outside reverse fold the neck at the shoulder – then outside reverse fold the head back again.

5
A

5
B

5
C

A
B

C

Now we must prepare the tail feathers from the *second* patterned sheet.

(**6**) Accordion fold the second sheet with alternate valley and mountain folds. Press the creases in firmly.

6

7

(**7**) When you have done that, valley fold the pleats in half. Put the fan in position on the Peacock's body and secure it with a little glue or double-sided tape. Glue the two centre parts of the tail fan together so that they hold their fan shape. If you like, you can also reverse fold the tail downwards to make a prop for the body

8

(**8**) There it is! A wonderful free-standing Peacock that looks beautiful left as an ornament around the house.

THE SWALLOW

This simple fold produces a bird from a water bomb base. Which just goes to prove that there is more than one way of skinning a cat! It recreates the tail design of the bird very cleverly, and allows us to employ a crimp fold at long last! Use a square of paper and fold it into a water bomb base.

(**1**) Fold the left and right flaps into rabbit's ears following the valley and mountain folds illustrated. Repeat with the two flaps behind.

1 A

1 B

(**2**) Mountain fold the model in half along its vertical centre line. Rotate the model 90° anticlockwise.

2

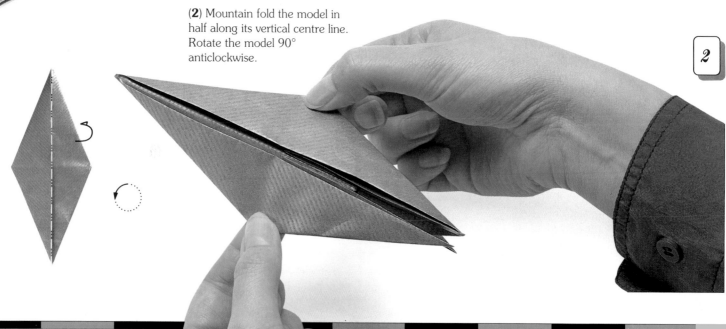

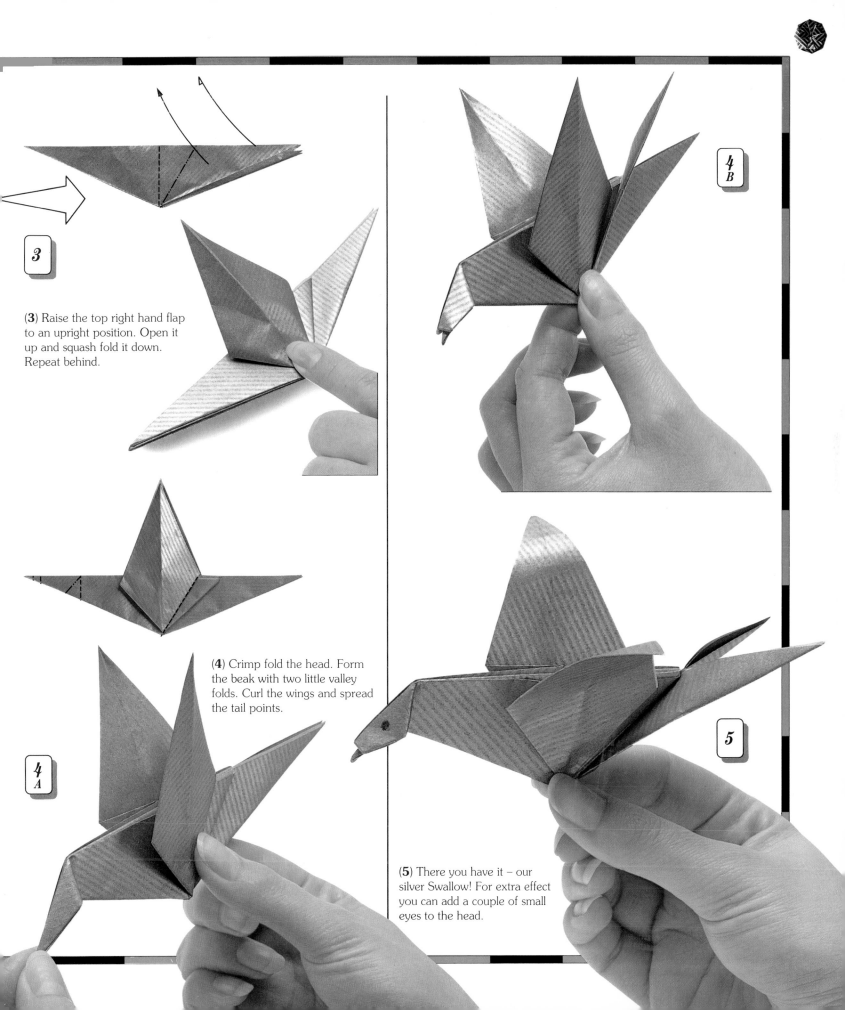

3

(**3**) Raise the top right hand flap to an upright position. Open it up and squash fold it down. Repeat behind.

**4
A**

(**4**) Crimp fold the head. Form the beak with two little valley folds. Curl the wings and spread the tail points.

**4
B**

5

(**5**) There you have it – our silver Swallow! For extra effect you can add a couple of small eyes to the head.

THE WOLF

A wolf in bird's clothing? Yes! This two-piece model starts off with a bird base for each component. Once you have mastered this fold, try altering the shape of the head, legs and tail and see if you can create a horse! You should find it relatively easy.

PART ONE (front legs, neck and head)

(**1**) Inside reverse fold both legs as far as the horizontal.

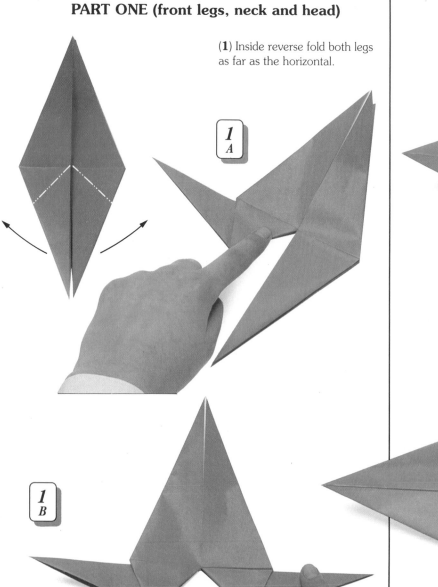

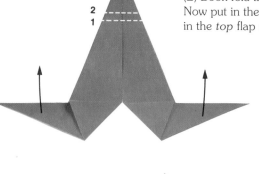

(**2**) Book fold them both open. Now put in the two valley folds in the *top* flap only.

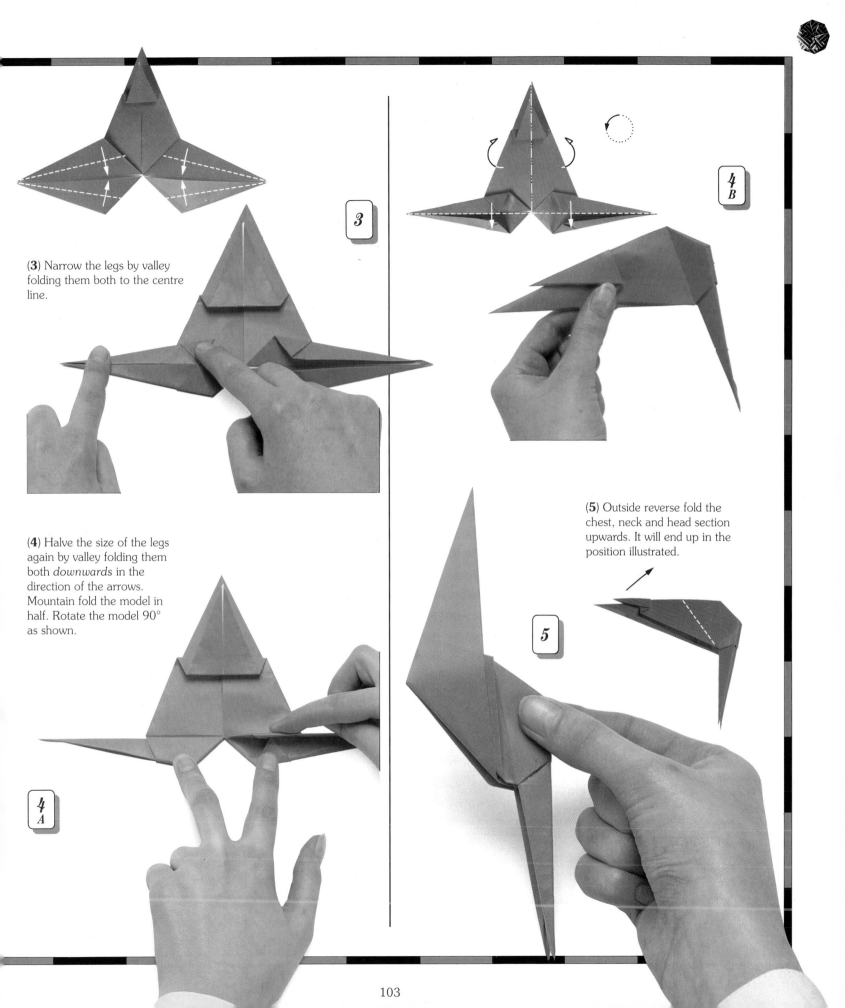

(**3**) Narrow the legs by valley folding them both to the centre line.

3

4
B

(**4**) Halve the size of the legs again by valley folding them both *downwards* in the direction of the arrows. Mountain fold the model in half. Rotate the model 90° as shown.

4
A

(**5**) Outside reverse fold the chest, neck and head section upwards. It will end up in the position illustrated.

5

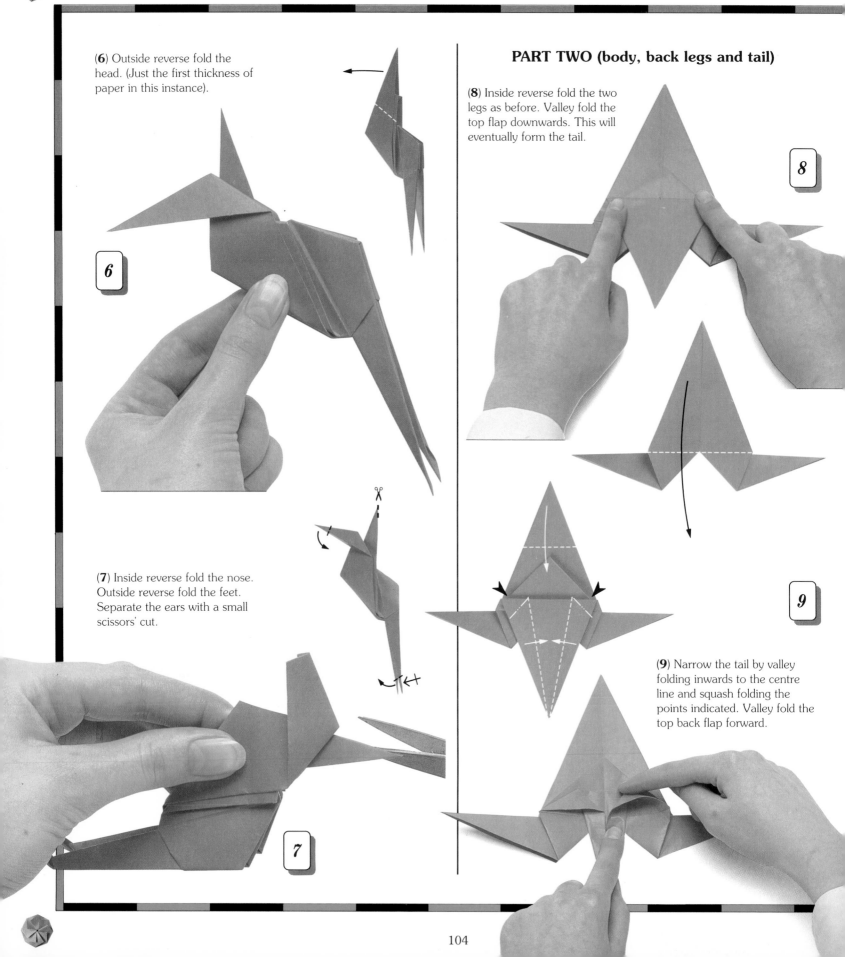

(**6**) Outside reverse fold the head. (Just the first thickness of paper in this instance).

6

(**7**) Inside reverse fold the nose. Outside reverse fold the feet. Separate the ears with a small scissors' cut.

7

PART TWO (body, back legs and tail)

(**8**) Inside reverse fold the two legs as before. Valley fold the top flap downwards. This will eventually form the tail.

8

9

(**9**) Narrow the tail by valley folding inwards to the centre line and squash folding the points indicated. Valley fold the top back flap forward.

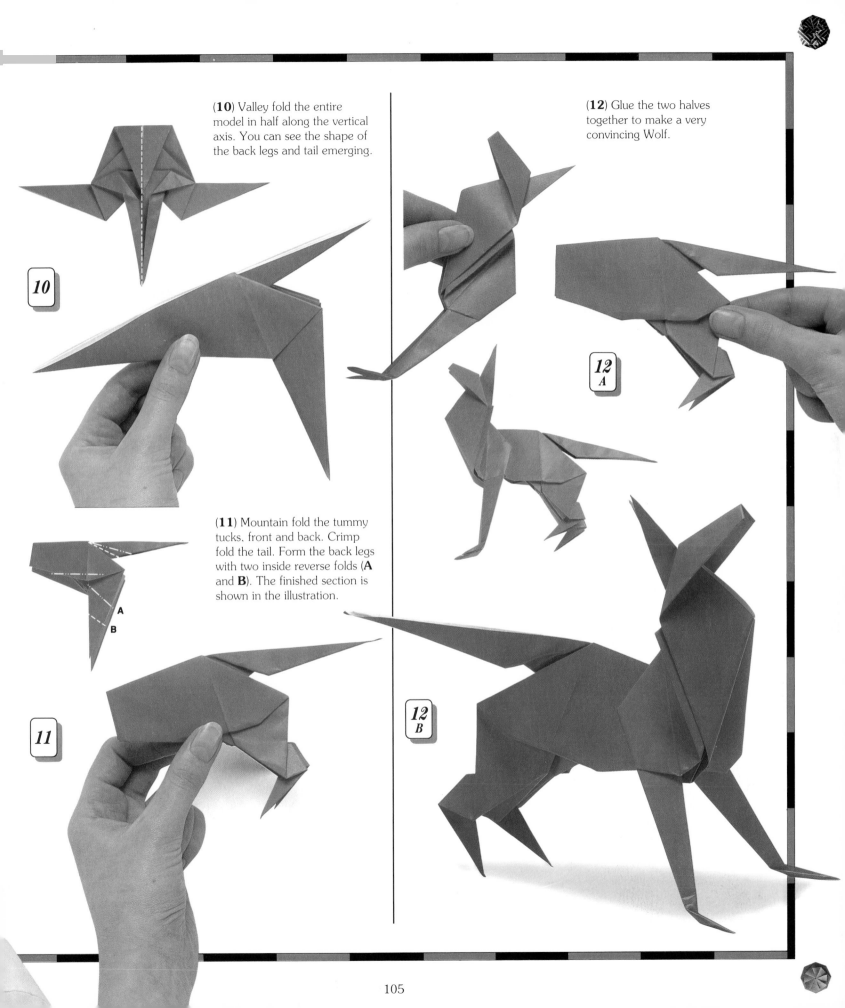

(**10**) Valley fold the entire model in half along the vertical axis. You can see the shape of the back legs and tail emerging.

10

(**11**) Mountain fold the tummy tucks, front and back. Crimp fold the tail. Form the back legs with two inside reverse folds (**A** and **B**). The finished section is shown in the illustration.

A
B

11

(**12**) Glue the two halves together to make a very convincing Wolf.

12 A

12 B

JUMPING FROG

This model hops about all over the place. It is quite difficult to fold, but take your time and you will get your just reward! Use a square that is large and, preferably, green. Use fairly thin paper so that the numerous folds do not get too fiddly. Start by folding a frog base.

(**1**) Book fold the frog base, front and back, revealing smooth surfaces.

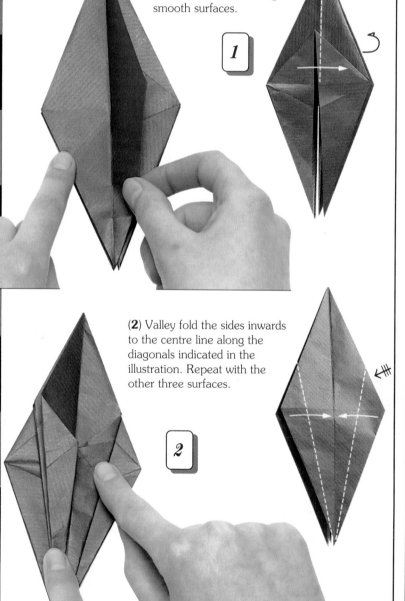

(**2**) Valley fold the sides inwards to the centre line along the diagonals indicated in the illustration. Repeat with the other three surfaces.

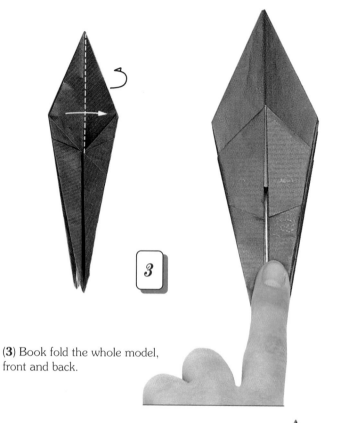

(**3**) Book fold the whole model, front and back.

(**4**) Inside reverse fold the lower points of the diamond shape to form the top two legs.

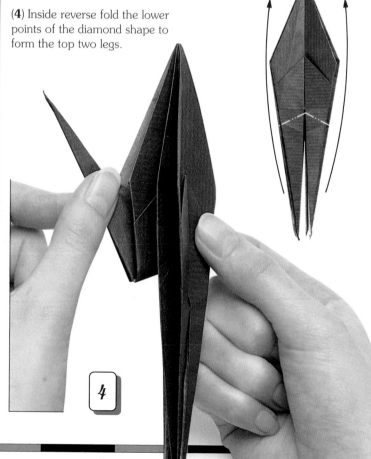

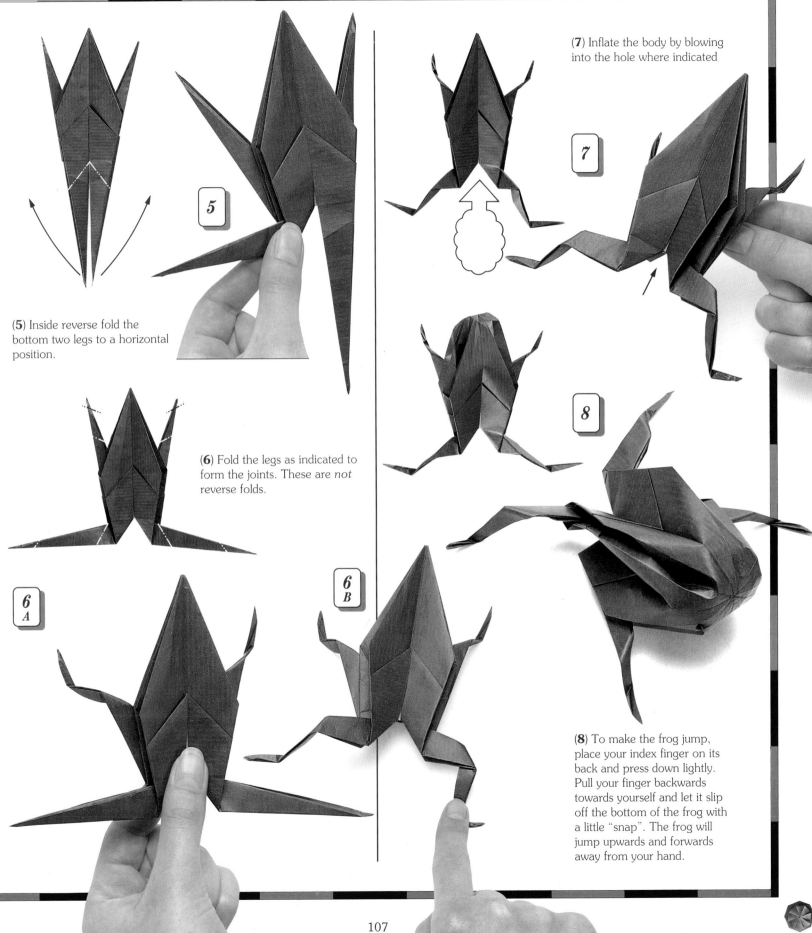

(5) Inside reverse fold the bottom two legs to a horizontal position.

5

(6) Fold the legs as indicated to form the joints. These are *not* reverse folds.

6 A

6 B

(7) Inflate the body by blowing into the hole where indicated

7

8

(8) To make the frog jump, place your index finger on its back and press down lightly. Pull your finger backwards towards yourself and let it slip off the bottom of the frog with a little "snap". The frog will jump upwards and forwards away from your hand.

THE SWAN

The Swan is probably the most beautiful bird in the world. Its elegant, graceful lines have delighted artists from the time immemorial. I am told that they make great eating too! People who live in the United Kingdom, like I do, will have to go abroad to experience that delicacy, however, because in our country they are a protected species, and nearly all belong to the Queen. She cannot stop us folding one though, can she? Use a square of white, or predominantly white, paper.

(**1**) Pre-crease the diagonal. Fold both sides to the centre line.

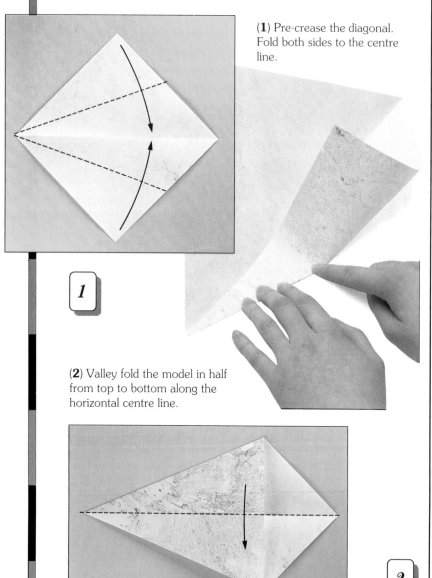

1

(**2**) Valley fold the model in half from top to bottom along the horizontal centre line.

2

(**3**) Valley fold the side upwards to align with the top horizontal. Repeat behind.

3

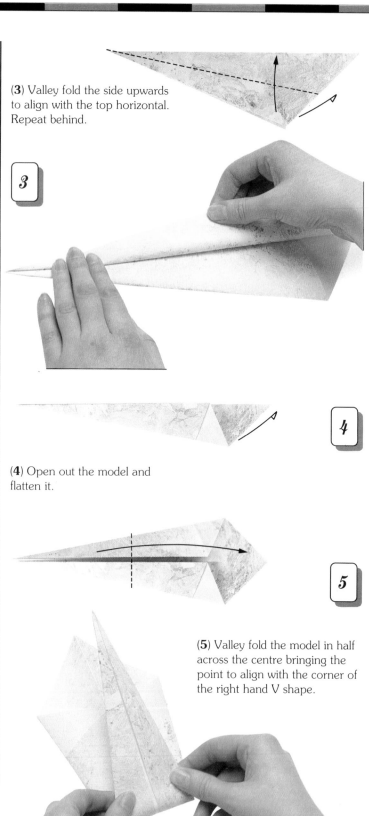

(**4**) Open out the model and flatten it.

4

5

(**5**) Valley fold the model in half across the centre bringing the point to align with the corner of the right hand V shape.

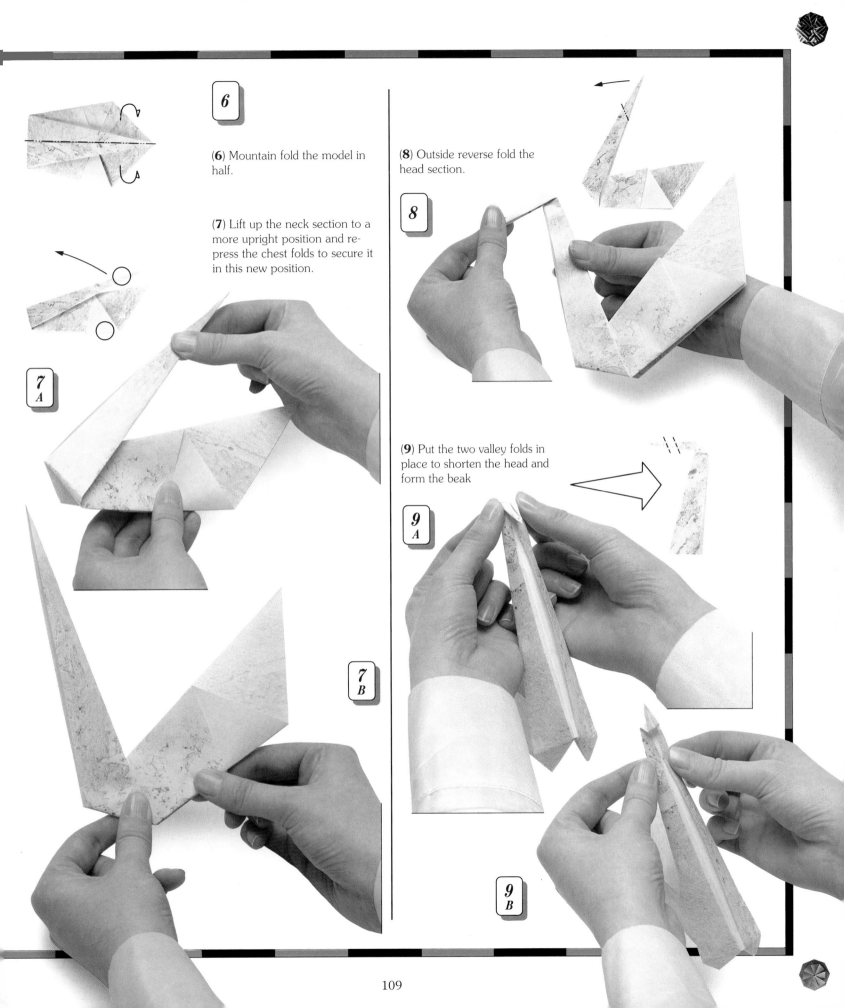

6

(**6**) Mountain fold the model in half.

(**7**) Lift up the neck section to a more upright position and re-press the chest folds to secure it in this new position.

7 A

7 B

(**8**) Outside reverse fold the head section.

8

(**9**) Put the two valley folds in place to shorten the head and form the beak

9 A

9 B

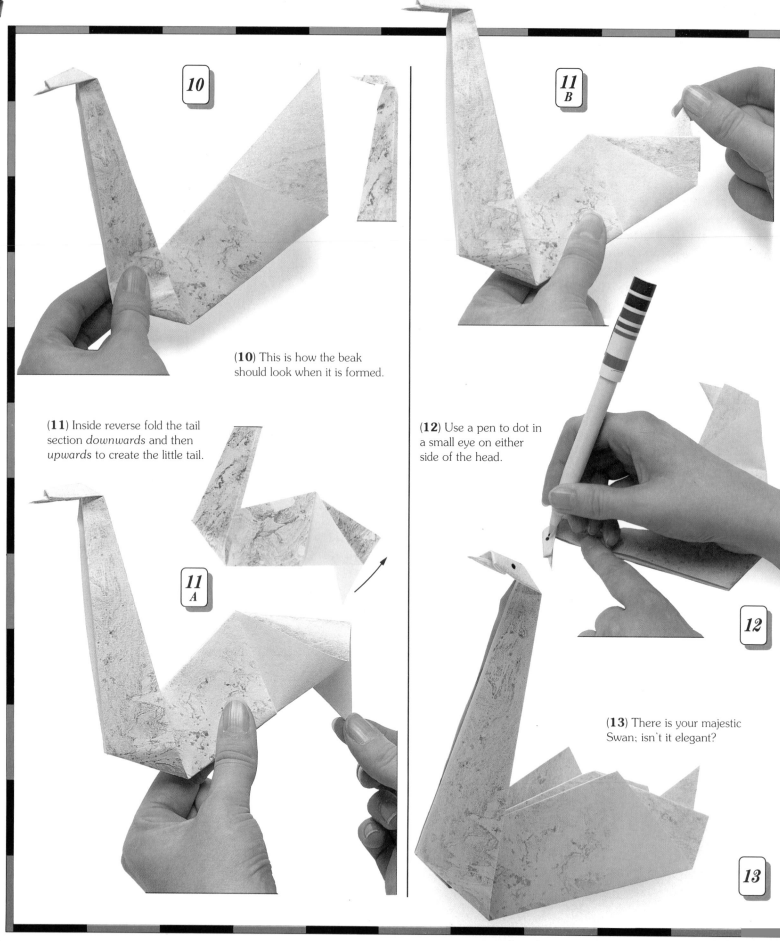

(**10**) This is how the beak should look when it is formed.

(**11**) Inside reverse fold the tail section *downwards* and then *upwards* to create the little tail.

(**12**) Use a pen to dot in a small eye on either side of the head.

(**13**) There is your majestic Swan; isn't it elegant?

THE GIRAFFE

Why have Giraffes got long necks? Because they can't stand the smell of their feet! Not a great joke, perhaps, but this is a great model. The fold, from a single square of paper, is quite remarkable. The old master's task was to create a model with four long legs, a long neck, two ears and a tail. No mean feat, I assure you! If you can find a paper with brown blotches or a mottled pattern, like this example, so much the better. If not, a plain light brown square will do. Start by folding a bird base. Have the points pointing upwards

(**1**) Valley fold the flaps down front and back.

1

(**2**) Valley fold the two right hand sections to the left, front and back.

2

(**3**) There are two points at the top. Outside reverse fold the top layer only at right angles to the rest of the model.

3

(**4**) Open out the main section by folding it to the right.

4

(**5**) Valley fold the top layers of the lower points of the kite shape to the centre line.

5

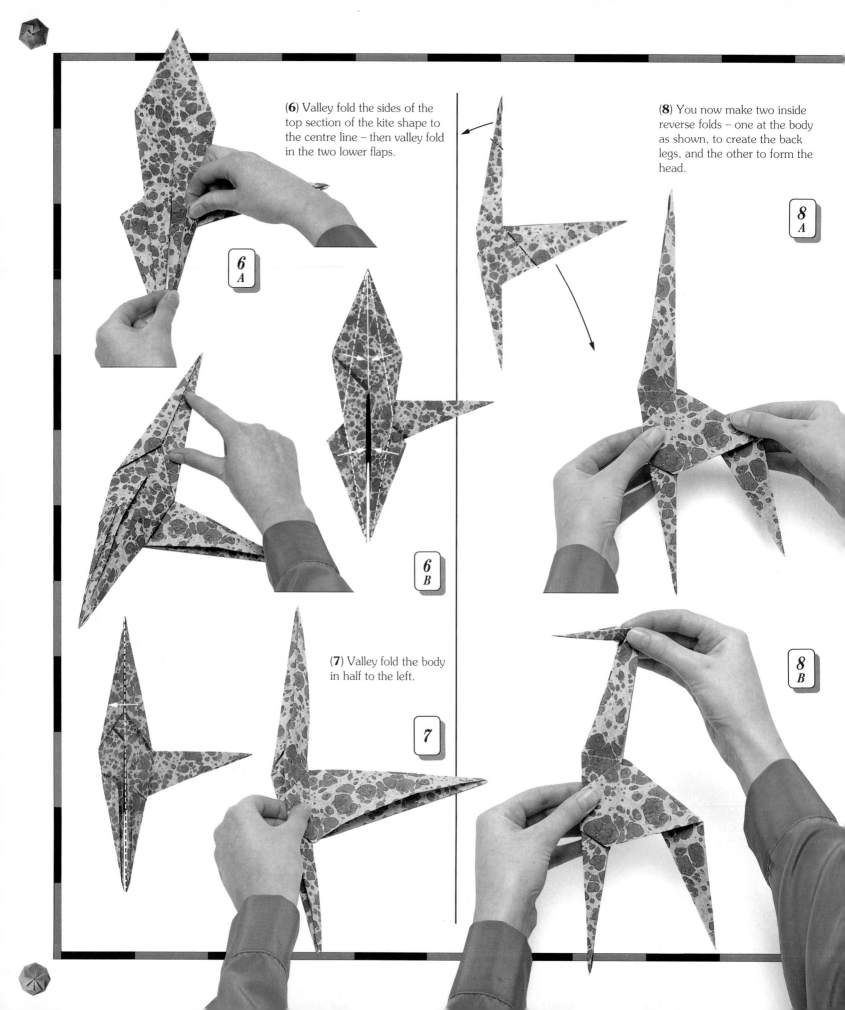

(**6**) Valley fold the sides of the top section of the kite shape to the centre line – then valley fold in the two lower flaps.

6 A

6 B

(**7**) Valley fold the body in half to the left.

7

(**8**) You now make two inside reverse folds – one at the body as shown, to create the back legs, and the other to form the head.

8 A

8 B

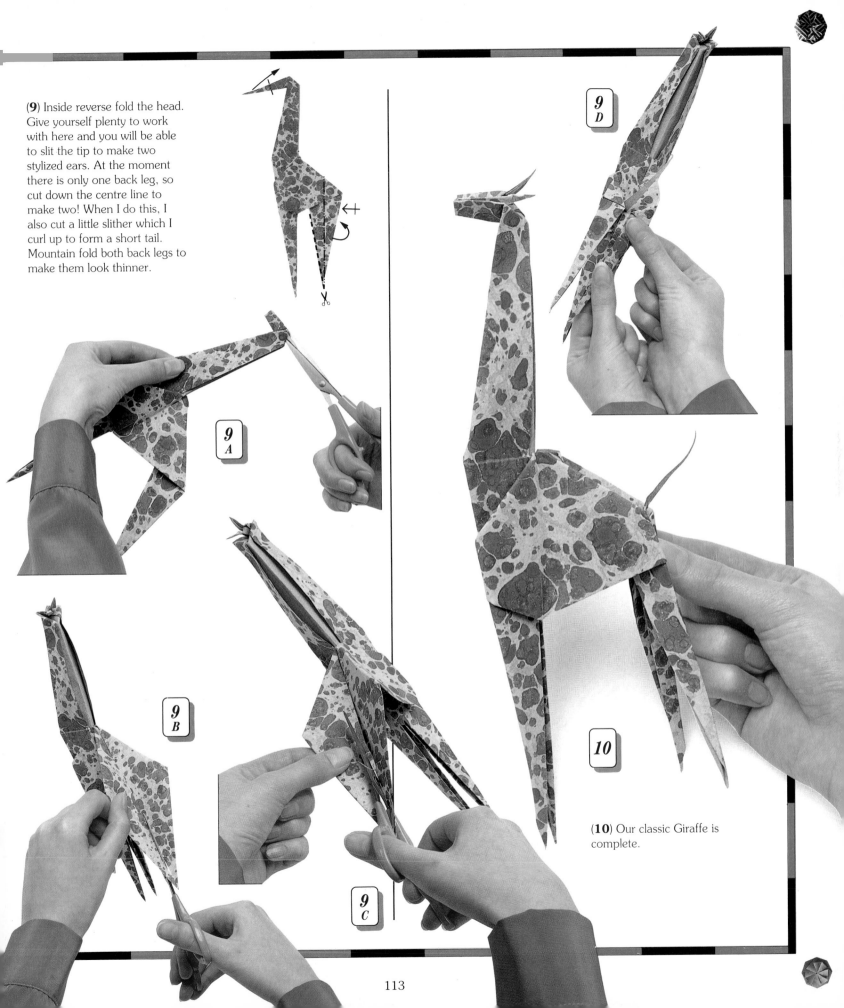

(**9**) Inside reverse fold the head. Give yourself plenty to work with here and you will be able to slit the tip to make two stylized ears. At the moment there is only one back leg, so cut down the centre line to make two! When I do this, I also cut a little slither which I curl up to form a short tail. Mountain fold both back legs to make them look thinner.

9
A

9
B

9
C

9
D

10

(**10**) Our classic Giraffe is complete.

THE FALCON

Have you seen birds of prey hovering motionless high above a grassy bank? Intent on their prey, their heads down and wings widely spread, they seem to hang in the air. It is a magnificent sight. It inspired me to create the next fold. Use a square of paper. If you are able to find a pattern that resembles a hawk's plumage, so much the better. Start with a bird base.

1

(**1**) Pull the two inside flaps outwards as far as they will go.

2

(**2**) Bring the two points together at the top and at the same time push the centre pointed section downwards following the mountain folds indicated. Fold flat. This is called a stretched bird base.

3

(**3**) Lift the left flap upright. Open it up from the outside edge, and *squash fold* it outwards. Repeat with the right flap.

4

(**4**) Mountain fold the model along the vertical centre line. Rotate the model 90° anticlockwise

5

(**5**) Lift the upper wing upwards and squash fold it into the new position following the mountain and valley folds shown. Repeat with the other wing.

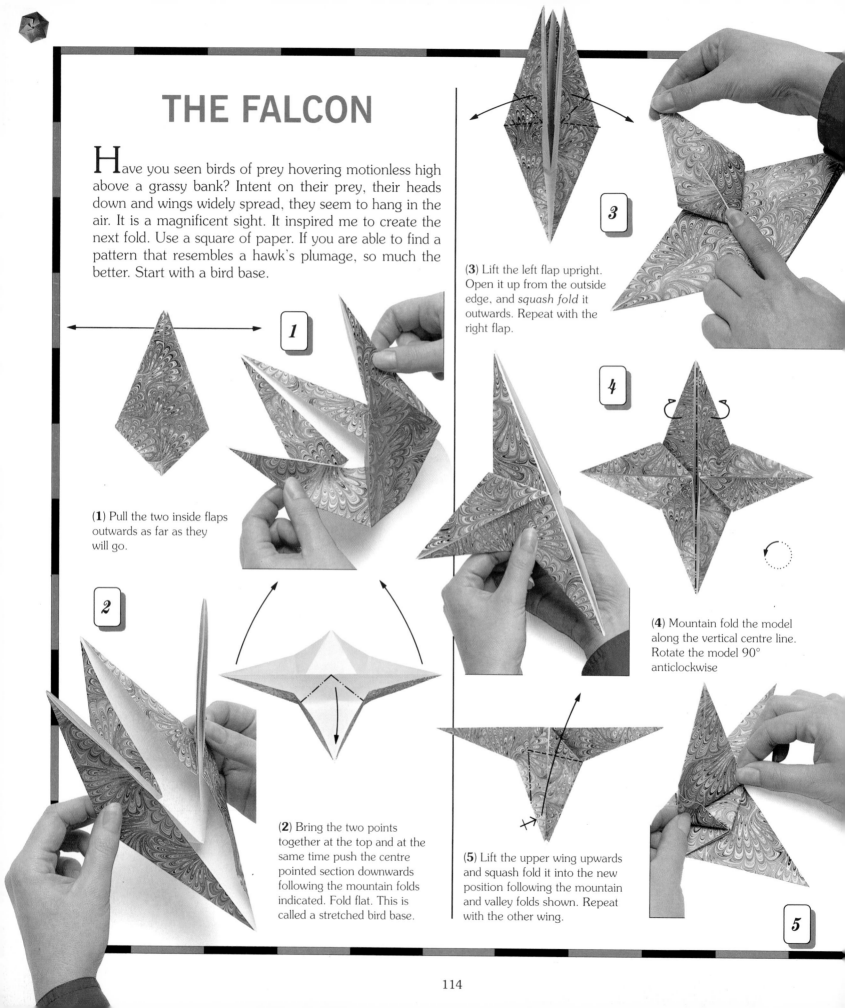

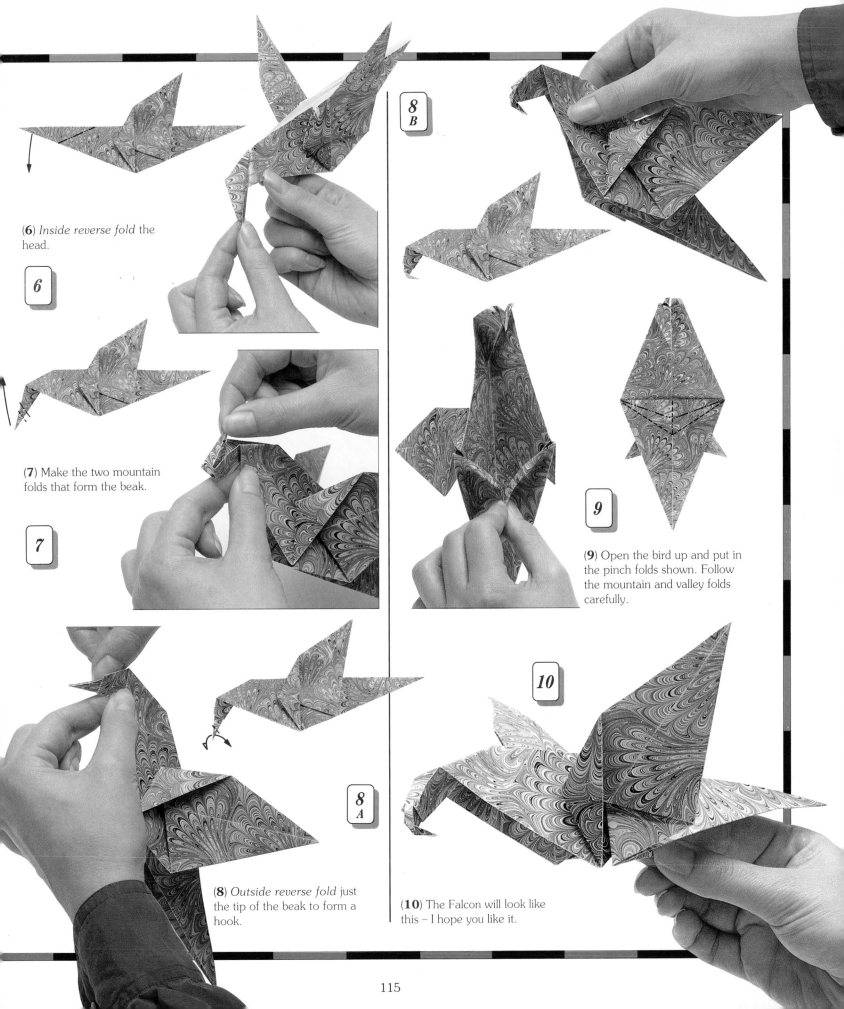

(**6**) *Inside reverse fold* the head.

6

(**7**) Make the two mountain folds that form the beak.

7

(**8**) *Outside reverse fold* just the tip of the beak to form a hook.

**8
A**

**8
B**

9

(**9**) Open the bird up and put in the pinch folds shown. Follow the mountain and valley folds carefully.

10

(**10**) The Falcon will look like this – I hope you like it.

THE HORSE

This is another two-piece model – another fine example of traditional simplicity. I first encountered it as a design printed on the back of a pack of Japanese origami paper. I liked it so much I filed it away for future reference – and here it is! Use two squares of paper of the same colour or pattern.

THE NECK AND HEAD

(**1**) Make an "ice-cream cone" shape with two valley folds – then mountain fold the unit in half along the horizontal axis.

(**2**) Squash fold the two sides following the mountain and valley folds indicated.

(**3**) Mountain fold the model in half down its vertical centre line.

(**4**) Outside reverse fold the first layer of paper to form the basis of the head.

(**5**) Inside reverse fold the ear section. This cleverly creates *two* ears out of one. Magic! Inside reverse fold the nose, as illustrated.

(**6**) Inside reverse fold the right point of this ear unit. This fold creates nicely pointed ears. Study the difference between (**6**) and (**7**) to see how the head profile changes.

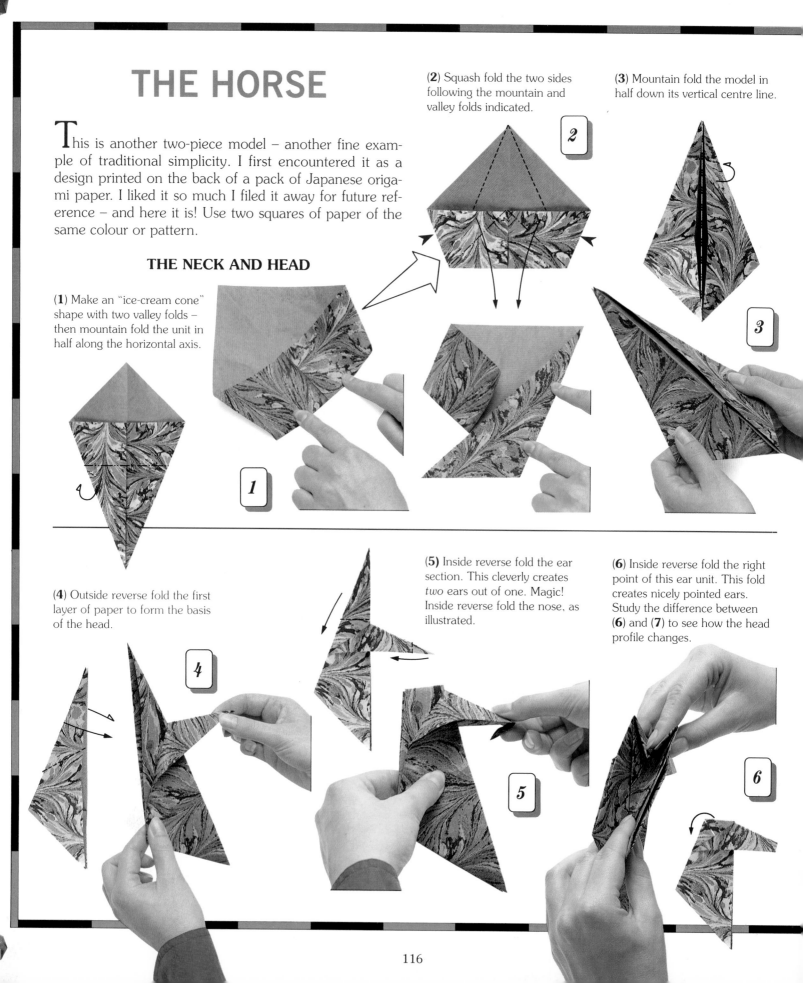

(7) Valley fold the mane. Repeat behind.

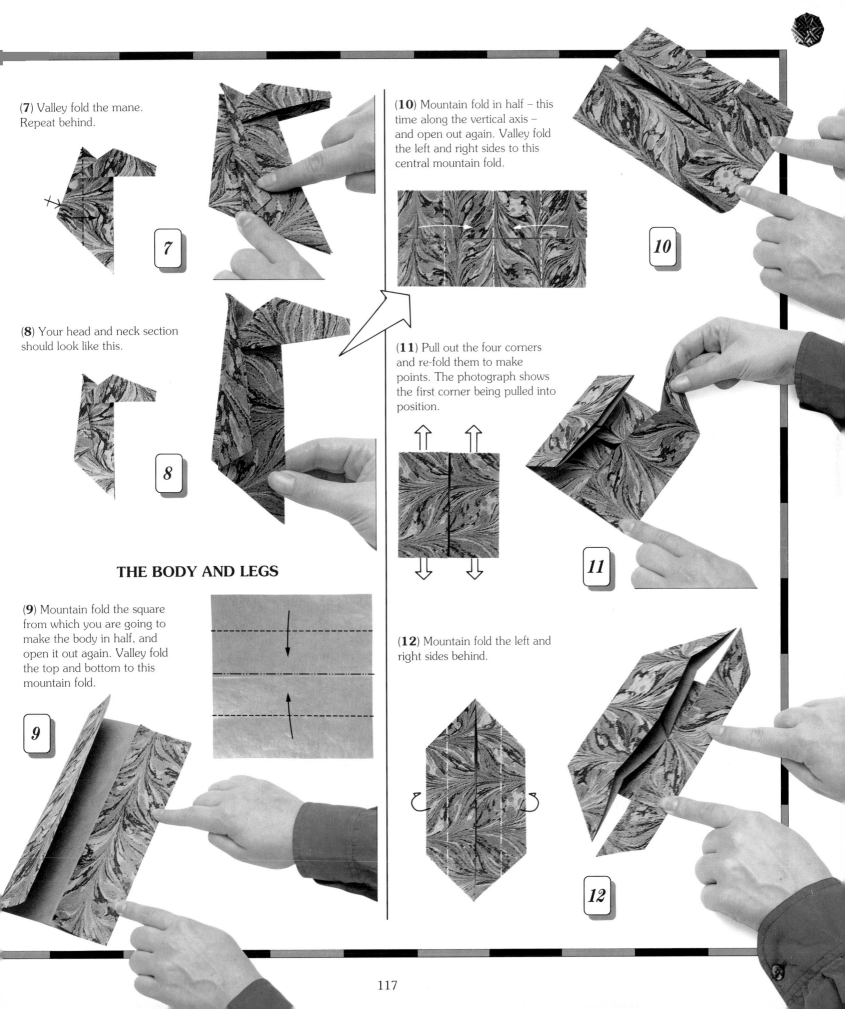

7

(8) Your head and neck section should look like this.

8

THE BODY AND LEGS

(9) Mountain fold the square from which you are going to make the body in half, and open it out again. Valley fold the top and bottom to this mountain fold.

9

(10) Mountain fold in half – this time along the vertical axis – and open out again. Valley fold the left and right sides to this central mountain fold.

10

(11) Pull out the four corners and re-fold them to make points. The photograph shows the first corner being pulled into position.

11

(12) Mountain fold the left and right sides behind.

12

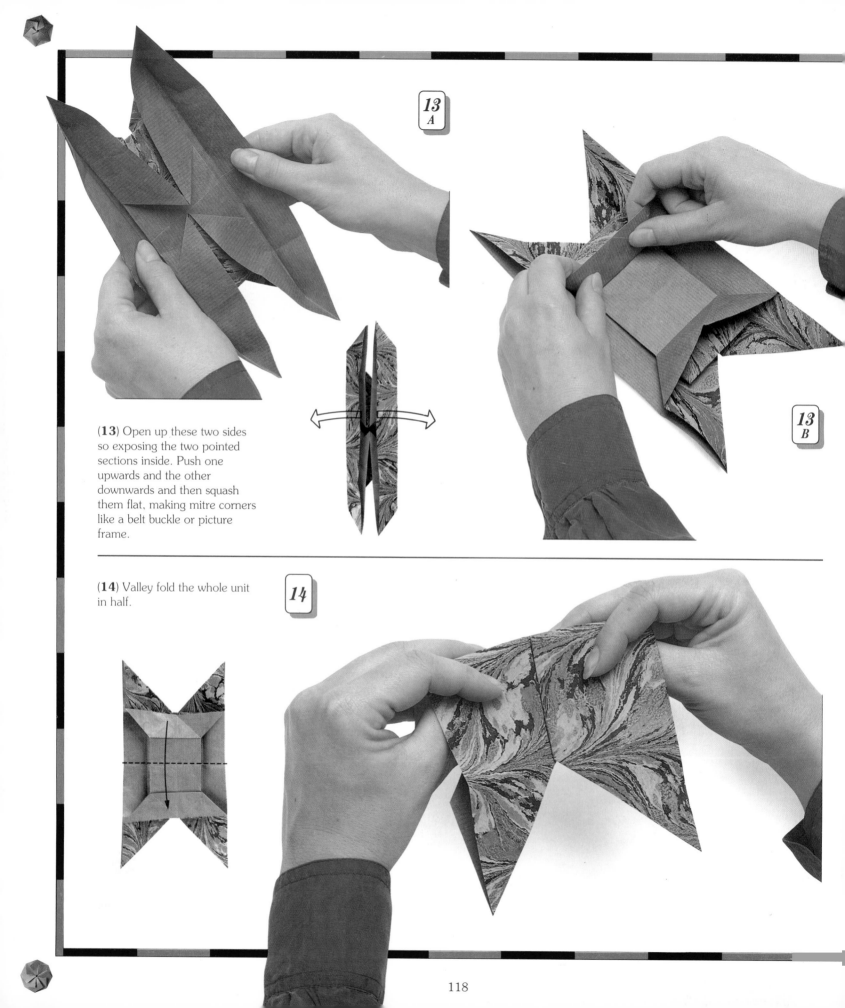

(**13**) Open up these two sides so exposing the two pointed sections inside. Push one upwards and the other downwards and then squash them flat, making mitre corners like a belt buckle or picture frame.

(**14**) Valley fold the whole unit in half.

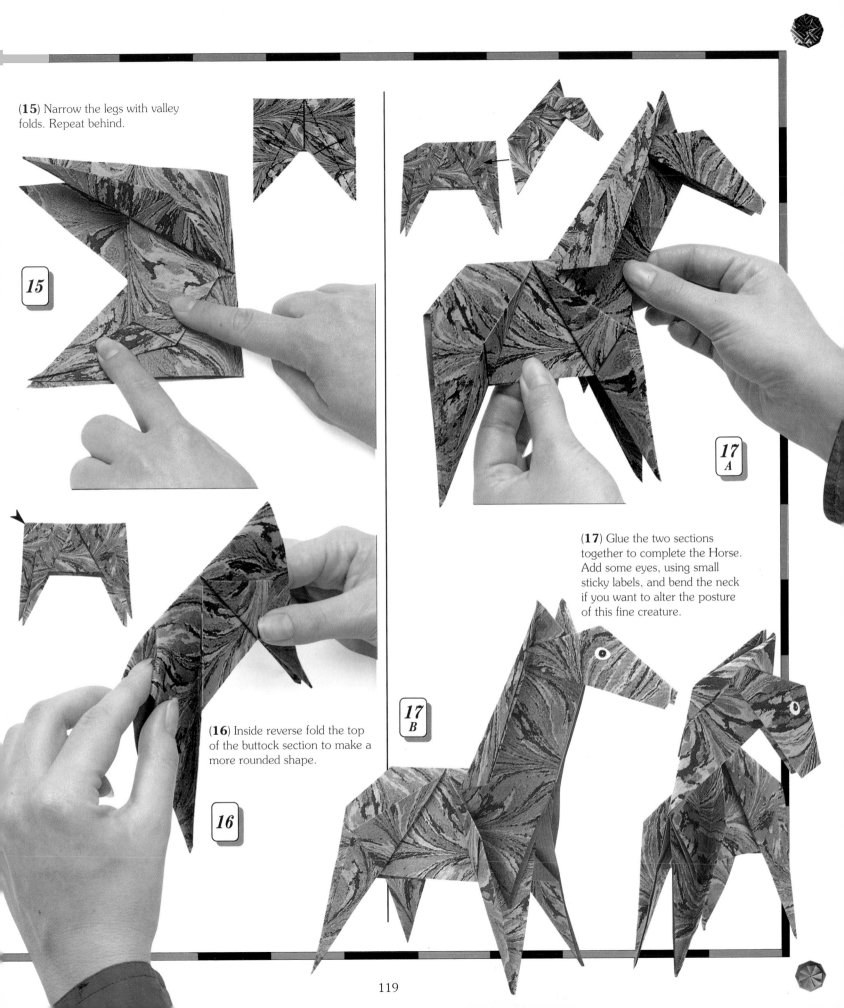

(**15**) Narrow the legs with valley folds. Repeat behind.

15

(**16**) Inside reverse fold the top of the buttock section to make a more rounded shape.

16

17
A

(**17**) Glue the two sections together to complete the Horse. Add some eyes, using small sticky labels, and bend the neck if you want to alter the posture of this fine creature.

17
B

FLOPPY EARS

I hope you have fun with this original fold and do not find it too difficult. Try to find paper that is coloured on one side and white on the other. The white side is important as it is used to create the impression of teeth and eyes. I have used scissors to form the big ears, buck teeth and eyes, which purists may dislike, but I consider the overall effect worth that liberty. Use a square and start with a bird base.

1 (**1**) Cut the *top flap* only along the line shown, as far as indicated. Turn the model over.

(**2**) Make a small scissors' cut in this flap.

2

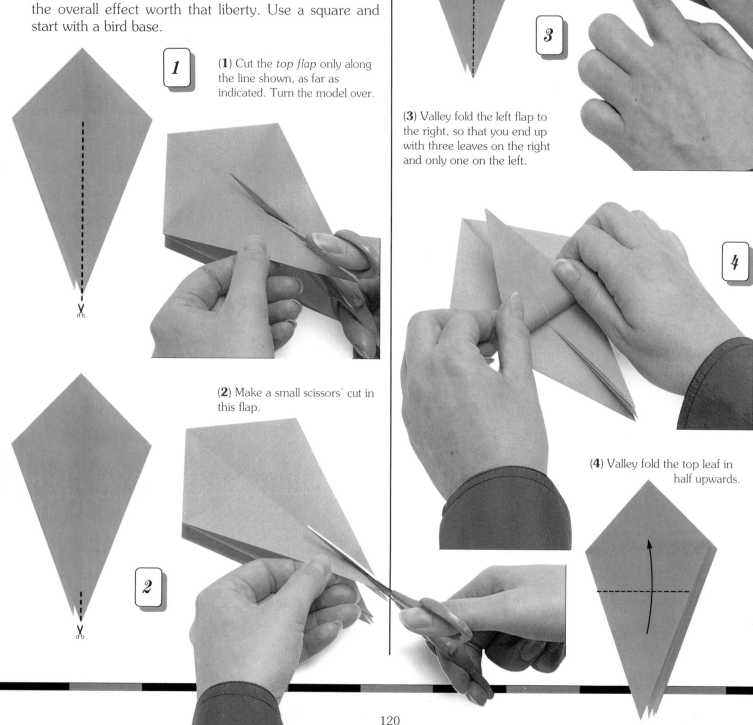

(**3**) Valley fold the left flap to the right, so that you end up with three leaves on the right and only one on the left.

3

4

(**4**) Valley fold the top leaf in half upwards.

(5) Open up and squash fold this upper section downwards, following the mountain and valley folds shown.

(7) Valley fold the tip of the white section upwards.

(6) Valley fold the sides of this section inwards to the centre line.

(8) Valley fold the right side of the entire model to the left.

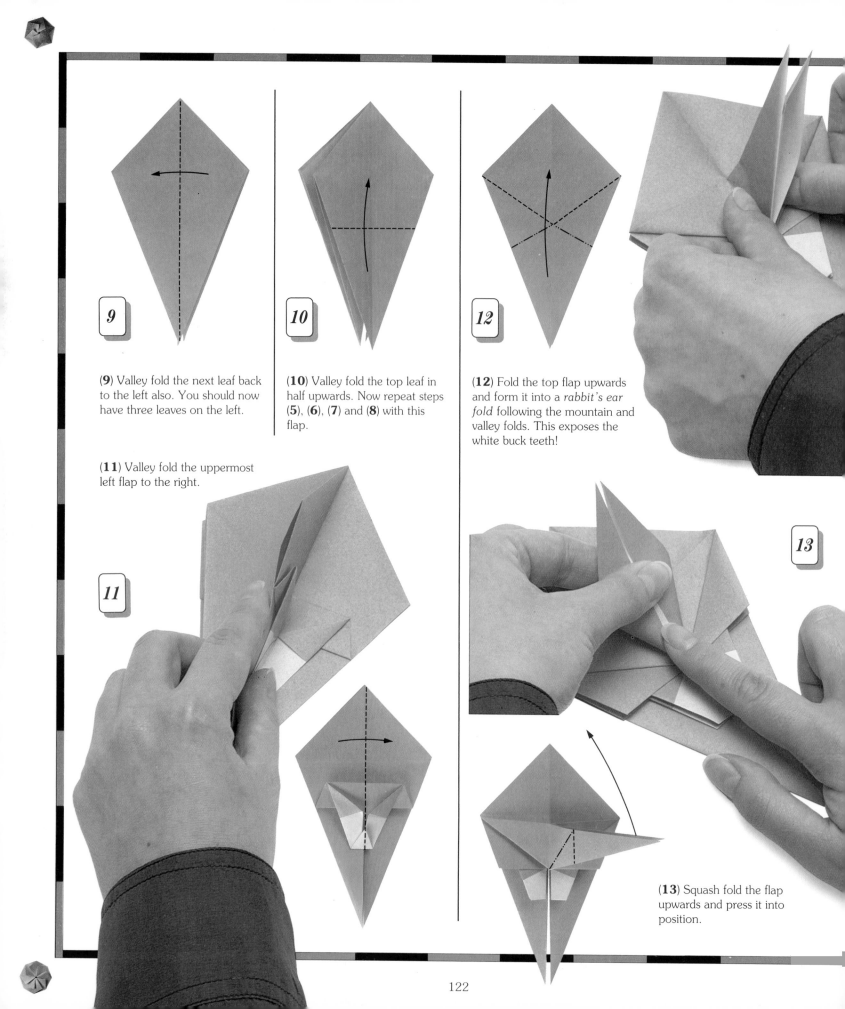

(**9**) Valley fold the next leaf back to the left also. You should now have three leaves on the left.

(**10**) Valley fold the top leaf in half upwards. Now repeat steps (**5**), (**6**), (**7**) and (**8**) with this flap.

(**11**) Valley fold the uppermost left flap to the right.

(**12**) Fold the top flap upwards and form it into a *rabbit's ear fold* following the mountain and valley folds. This exposes the white buck teeth!

(**13**) Squash fold the flap upwards and press it into position.

(14) This point already has a small cut in it. Make two more cuts being careful to *snip only the upper surfaces of these tips*. Now open them out left and right.

(15) Mountain fold where shown and tuck the flap down into the pocket, leaving just two little white triangles sticking out.

(16) These little triangles become the pupils of the eyes. Valley fold the tips, making these folds just long enough so that the *extreme tips* tuck down into the pocket below.

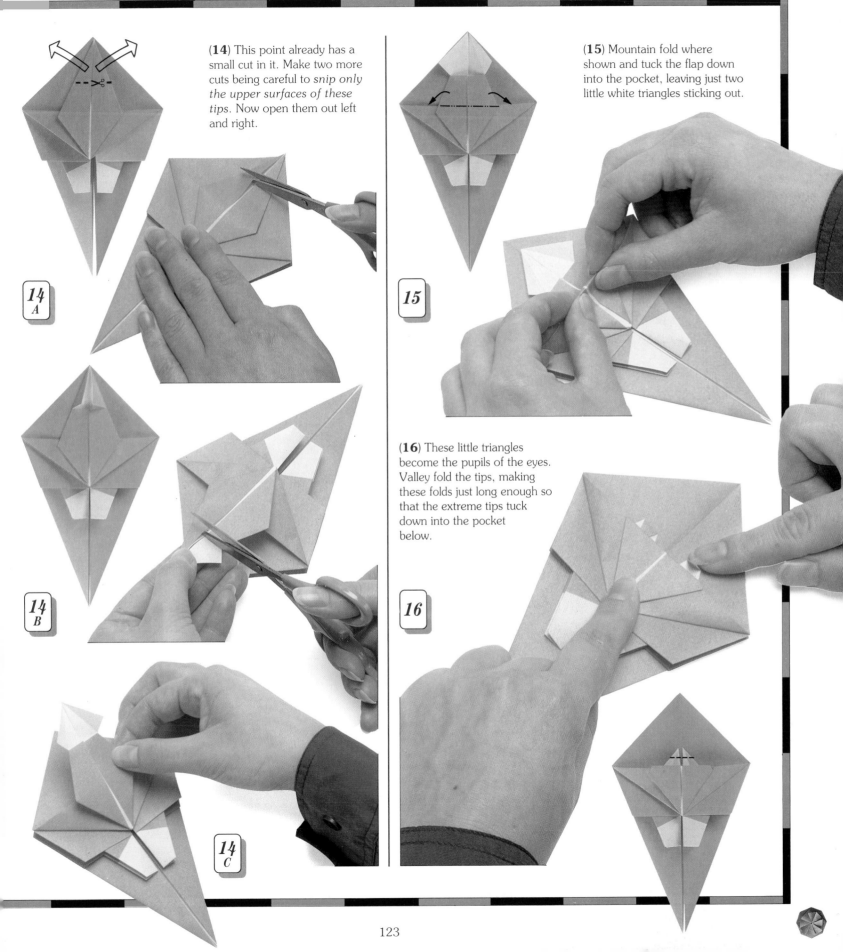

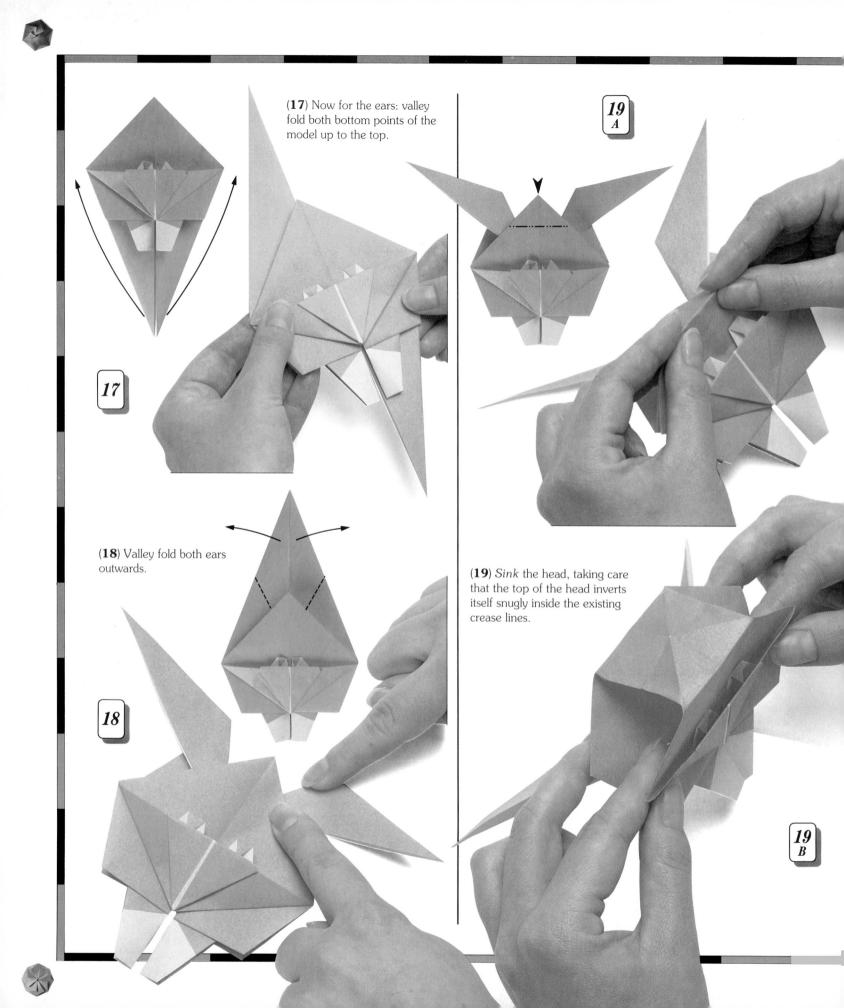

(**17**) Now for the ears: valley fold both bottom points of the model up to the top.

17

(**18**) Valley fold both ears outwards.

18

19
A

(**19**) *Sink* the head, taking care that the top of the head inverts itself snugly inside the existing crease lines.

19
B

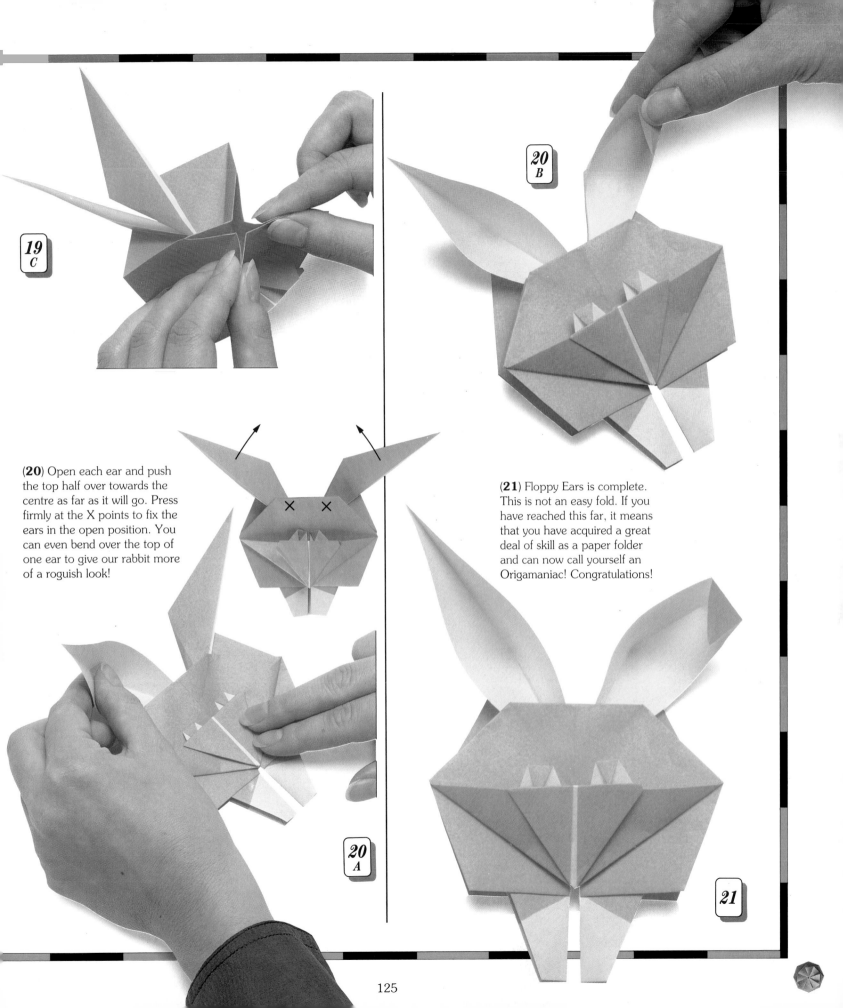

19 C

20 B

(**20**) Open each ear and push the top half over towards the centre as far as it will go. Press firmly at the X points to fix the ears in the open position. You can even bend over the top of one ear to give our rabbit more of a roguish look!

(**21**) Floppy Ears is complete. This is not an easy fold. If you have reached this far, it means that you have acquired a great deal of skill as a paper folder and can now call yourself an Origamaniac! Congratulations!

20 A

21